Going to War; Back from War

To all of you, who don't know me or even heard of me. I am Alton E. Pete, U.S. Army, retired. Throughout my military career of serving and protecting our country for the safety and the freedom of the American people. I did my dangerous and in harm's way tour while in Iraq.

When I say, harm's way! We were walking and fighting many days of being in harm's way until we have to learn how to get out of the way. Those mortar rounds and those repeated fire fights wasn't any joke. This was for real!

Wounds, that are taking years to heal. The silent ones and the physical ones are sounding off every day! What we've done for our country speaks high volume and will not be forgotten. It's history like a mystery for our liberty...

Life Is So Precious

Life Is So Precious

Alton Eugene Pete
United States Army, Retired

Library of Congress Control Number: 2016911138
ISBN: Hardcover   978-1-5245-2423-4
               Softcover   978-1-5245-2424-1
               eBook   978-1-5245-2425-8

Print information available on the last page.

Rev. date: 03/27/2017

To order additional copies of this book, contact:
Xlibris
1-888-795-4274
www.Xlibris.com
Orders@Xlibris.com
744212

The Phrases and Quotes:

Life is so precious
I have enough courage, confidence, and the faith to say, I refuse to lose and
accept defeat......

Life is hopeful, delightful, beautiful, incredible, lovable, teachable, joyful,
powerful, faithful, enjoyable, reachable, gentle, passionate, encouraging,
exciting, romantic, unlimited, positive, glorious, compassionate, tender, full
of Liberty, inspirational, motivational, kind, precious, adventurous, full of
happiness, strong, firm, full of surprises, holy, amazing, and ordained by God.

Just like the morning sun is rising into shining for the day. It rises above a good day and a bad day, it rises above a sunny day and a rainy day. It rises above the failures, the disappointments, the shame and the pride. It rises above the happiness and the sadness. It rises above the joy, the sorrow and for a better tomorrow. Then, when the day has ended the morning sun is prepared to rise the very next day to do it all over again. Nothing prevents the morning sun from rising into shining, no matter what comes and no matter what goes.

Don't stay where you are! Be prepared to get up, jump up and rise.....

Dreams and gifts are like the stars that come out at night.
There are so many, only God can count them and name them....

When the eagles, the hawks and other fowls of the air are ready for their little ones to grow up and be big ones.

They stop feeding them and from a distance the eagles, the hawks and the other fowls are watching their babies step to the edge of the nest to see when and how they are going to take flight and leave the nest. This is the only way the parents can encourage their babies to fly in the air and soar. The hunger to seek more does play a role.

Some may ask why and how come? The parents are doing this to their babies. The main reason is because the little babies are too big for the nest and perhaps the father birds had a talk with the mother birds and said; it's time to let our babies grow up, look how big they are.

What turns the little babies into responsible young adults is the hunger and the will to show their parents everything you've taught me and the way you've raised me has paid off. Sometimes something has to happen to bring the good out of you. So never give up, on you.

Children learn as much as you can from your parents. Be responsible and respectful young adults. Go after those positive things, your heart desires. Stay hungry, flap those wings and make your parents proud.

Life is going to confront you with a few, if not more pressured situations. I remember my mom telling us while growing up. When you find yourself wrestling with a bear and you don't defeat that bear, you are going to run into a lion.

What I have gotten out of that concept now that I'm a man. Is, that lion is watching you wrestle with the bear from a remote different position. Taking mental notes on how to wrestle with you as well. So, you've got to find a way to win over that bear because the lion is waiting too.

It doesn't matter what kind of pressure is knocking at your door. I would rather have the favor of God more than anything else in this world to get me through any pressured situations. He's the only one who can open up some new doors and open up some new windows from the old doors and the old windows that have closed in our face while running in this race.

Pressure is design to change you and to define you, make you stronger to last longer. Don't run from it, run through it....

Fellas, all the men need to hear this. A woman will follow our lead after learning and watching the way we treat ourselves.

Always treat that special lady in your life, the same identical way that you treat and love your own self.

Our women are Queens every single day. Even on the weekends she deserves to be treated and respected as such.

Men don't be afraid to express your love to the lady you are in love with. Remember she's going to treat you, love you and respect you the same way in return....express your unconditional love today.

Whatever kind of way and however kind of way you've built your house. You have to learn how to cherish and live in the house you've built.

Soon if not later! You may have to do some renovations, you may have to do some remodeling and you may have to make a few changes along the way.

Whatever you do, be faithful and be a good keeper over your own house. You've built it...

Someone gave word to Jesus at a wedding, we have ran out of wine. Jesus says go bring me some buckets of water and be sure they are filled up to the top. He said, I will wave my hand across the buckets and we'll have some wine to drink. Before that wedding was over, there was some wine to drink during the ceremony of a celebration.

Today, if anyone has ran out of faith, hope, love, peace, joy, happiness, trust, strength, forgiveness, ways of controlling your temper. And are still hurting with pain from previous relationships, friendships and family matters. Speak to Jesus and give him a word and watch him wave his hand across whatever you ask him to do.

It will be done! Rejoice and start celebrating.....

Enjoy the sunshine like the rain...they both promote your growth! Sometimes when the good comes from good, what's so good about it? Similar to the rich receiving back from the rich, what's so rich about it? When the good derives from something horrible, terrible and so bad. This is the best kind of Good, to attain.

When people mistreat you! Be strong enough to walk away and count it all joy. Anyone who laughs first at you, will end up laughing last...the first will be last and the last will be first! There is no need to prove anything to anyone when you know, who you are and secured within your heart and soul.

There is so much more of the good things waiting ahead for us, than what has been left behind....keep looking ahead to chase those goals!

Greater sooner or Greater later, which ever one comes first for you!

When the old leaves have fallen from your tree in order to start a cold and a wet season. This kind of change plays a pivotal role and can cause one to feel empty on the outside and sometimes on the inside. The new leaves will come right on time to restore the loss from the old leaves of your tree in order to start a warm and a sunny season. This is how, when and why we all get a fresh new beginning for our strong standing tree.

You are stronger than you think you are!

There are two types of selfishness among people. The good selfishness is when someone or others are trying to get themselves together by blocking out all nonsense and doesn't mind seeing others make it too. The bad kind of selfishness is when someone or others thinks about themselves only and doesn't care about anyone else or anything else. Which one of the two describes you? When one person hurt, we all should hurt. What the first person get the last person should get it too. When another person smile, we all should smile. When someone else makes it, we all should get on board and make it. The point is, try to be more inviting and more lovingly towards each other.

It's always nice to be nice.

Don't be afraid to get paid. Get yours!

We all are soldiers! We don't make excuses, we find a way and we make things happen. How does anyone become better unless you learn from your mistakes? The older and mature we become the less mistakes we make to become better.

You can recognize a very romantic individual with love, not because the days are looking good. But, when the years have passed and the love is romancing, flowing and rowing like the waters of the sea, smooth and easy. You can hear a true singer, not because the music is playing and the band is jamming. But, when the music stops and the singer is singing a style of Acapella that sounds, so good.

Contents

When the darkness of life has covered your world; it's just a test, it's for a short season. People may leave you and even walk away, but it's ok. Cause you to fold up your tent and quit. This is the time to gather yourself, find yourself and get yourself together. Remember, God is still able to keep you from going crazy, he's able to keep you from loosing your mind and he's able to deliver you back, safe in his arms.....''Don't know when and how, but Great things are coming your way''. The dust floating around in the air will settle, for you to see clearly again...

Therefore, you are going to achieve your expectations. There is no room or space for doubt. There is no need to fear, when God is walking on your water towards you. No need to be afraid, when God is knocking on your door, let him in. No need to be despaired or discouraged, when God is climbing right beside you, on your hills and your mountains. No need to be dismayed or distressed, when God is walking in front of you, leading you out of your valley. You are going to make it, you are going to be alright and you are going to come out of whatever it is, that's holding you up or holding you down......

There is hope; this is for everyone, the blessings that come from God are not just for the Bishops, the Deacons, the Pastors or the singer with the anointing on a Sunday morning. God still chooses and uses ordinary people as well.

It doesn't matter how high the rank we achieve throughout our military careers or on that corporate job making one the CEO. God doesn't have any respect of person, simply because he can raise up anyone for his glory; it's not over, it's the start of your new beginning....

That woman, who was very sick for so many years. Perhaps, tried every doctor in town and they all, just let her down. This same woman hears about the miracles and probably seen others healed and delivered as well. But, this time around she wanted to touch, feel and witness for her self. Her mind was made up and her heart was in the right connection with her spirit, regardless who was pressing against Jesus and attacking her at the same time. She wanted to touch and feel for her self, she wasn't going to stop, quit or give up. With sincerity, perseverance and the faith that woman got everything and more from the Lord. So, Jesus felt her pain, saw her need and fulfilled her desire.

The vital lesson to take away from this true story is, it doesn't matter who don't want to see you make it, get blessed, get that home, get that CEO job, get that financial increase funded on your checking and savings account, or start up that billion dollar business. Regardless, who is pressing and attacking you, there is always someone or something that's going to be in your way, you have to make up in your mind, use your faith and persevere to get that touch and experience it all for yourself. It's yours, for the asking...

God is the only one, who can change lives, fix and repair lives and restore your life back together, like never before....

To my mother and my sister:
my sincere gratitude for believing in me. There is no one like you.
I yearn, everyday to hear the sound of my name from you two.
When the void and the emptiness has tried to rest in my heart over
the years; God has eased the sorrow into comforting me.....

People keep on asking, "Why do you keep on pushing?
You look so strong, you talk so strong—why do you keep on pushing?"
The Lord has given me the strength I need, the Lord has set me free

People keep on asking, "Why do you keep on singing?
You sound so good, you make me feel so good—why do you keep on singing?"
The Lord has been really good to me, gave me a song to sing

People keep on asking, "Why do you keep on teaching?
You have all of these degrees, you're always writing—
why do you keep on teaching?"
The Lord has smiled on me, gave me all the things I need.

Acknowledgments

This amazing book was created, inspired by, and left me compelled to write by the strength and the courage from my brothers Leon Pete and Pastor Phillip Pete. After everything we have experienced together, this has made us closer than the air we breathe.

To our mother, the late First Lady Mother, Lillian Pete, and our sister Yvette Pete—you two will never ever be forgotten. Thank you, Momma and Yvette, for always believing in me. I miss that part of you two beyond the imagination of anyone's wondering mind. To my father, thank you too.

Giving up was not anywhere near the Pete family vocabulary while you two were around, and it still remains that way today. Although, we may have been knocked down to our knees, the Lord has given us the strength that we need to rise again. Therefore, I will not allow pain to rule and follow me around like a shadow any longer. I will act as if this has never existed, while trying to avoid it like this has never happened, covering it up and hoping it will go away.

Dedication

I would like to personally dedicate this book to all the brokenhearted, all the families dealing with very strong difficult family issues. Not knowing how and where to look for your guidance, or finding someone to understand. Through the good times and the bad, you will and you shall get through your fiery furnace without any touch of fire burning up your skin, or even the smell of smoke on your clothes. We do need to remember, without God, we cannot get through any storm on our own. Jesus is our help. Learn to trust God with all your heart and try not to lean on your own understanding.

    I also dedicate this to all the hopeless, deeply depressed individuals, men and women behind the prison walls and all the children as well. We all have fallen down and fallen short of God's glory, but don't stay down. Get up out of your mess, get up from your dirt and mud because this will weigh you down. Get up out of your shame and embarrassment. Find a way to get up out of your troubles and learn to smile again. Learn to appreciate your life again. Rediscover your hopes and dreams again. Use your mind and follow your heart to create positive ideas again; after all, it's about doing the right thing so that you can sleep better at night and not be bothered with so much junk all night long.

For our youth

To all of our youth throughout this great country of the United States of America and overseas, who are approaching graduation or are getting ready to graduate from high school and transition from high school into what we all call, adulthood.

This part of your life is going to be challenging, new, unfamiliar, completely different and will leave you with some very difficult hard choices to make for the next phase of your life.

You are going to be facing decisions like, what to do next, where to go from here, what should you do to become a better person, how do you fit into the work place, what kind of career should you choose to do, while trying to discover who am I, what direction should you go, how to be independent, and simply making a name for yourself.

Take my advise, there are two choices in life to go: the first one is going in the right direction of doing things the right way, for a positive outcome. The second choice is doing things the wrong way and leading you into a path of going no where real quick and in a hurry. This kind of path I would recommend to avoid at all cost because there is no future, no career in it, and you will find yourself in jail or no longer around to enjoy this new phase of your journey.

I would like to pass on a few choices to decide on that is so expedient and self fulfilling to accomplish. If, the professional sports are out of your reach there are also some other promising careers, big dreams, trade schools, and professional occupations that will enhance your abilities to reach those high levels of success in your life. Your future is bright, awaiting for you to indulge in, to become the very best and nothing lest.

Join the military; there are several to select from; the Army, the Airforce, the Navy, the Marines and lastly the Coast Guard. These fantastic career moves will definitely provide all kinds of perfect opportunities to learn about yourself, develop positive skills and working habits, build inner strength, sharpen your mind, and learn more about life that your parents didn't teach you, to explore the world and to see so many unique places that you have never seen before. Bottom line, the military will help you structure your life and become better as a person, that's guaranteed.

You will grow up to be responsible mature adults and learn who you are from the training provided. The military can teach you how to budget your finances, how to keep your credit scores in good standings, how to be accountable and trustful with millions of dollars worth of equipment. The military can teach you how to build a family away from home, how to be neat and how to stay healthy along with the many various exercising programs that are shared among all the branches. Plus the benefits are remarkable and are worth joining the military for. You will have the pleasure of learning from the best qualified experienced men and women from all branches wearing the uniform. Anything you can imagine to be and want to do in the military, you can achieve.

Not ready for the military; attend college get some degrees next to your name and become a judge, become a doctor, become a music artist, become a professor, become a CEO, become an attorney, become a Senator, become a Governor, become a Mayor, start your own professional business and become a millionaire.

Whatever, you decide to be and decide to do; do not wast your life by getting any felonies, getting into any trouble with the law, do not disrespect your parents you'll never know more than them. When you start getting off track find yourself quickly and get back on track. Do not start having babies you'll have all the time you need down the road to get married and start a family once you are financially established and able to raise a family.

Now, I know we want the best for our children, I know we want our children to hurry up and grow up. But, what ever happened to allowing our children to grow up in the kitchen and teaching them how to cook, showing them how to wash the dishes, and how to take out the trash when it gets too full to put any more trash in the trash can. What ever happened to showing them how to wash their clothes separating the color clothes from the white clothes instead of shopping for more new clothes at the mall. What ever happened to showing them how to cut the grass in the front yard and the back yard instead of watching the grass grow higher than the fence surrounding the whole house.

What ever happened to telling our children to sit still and you better not move, when you're out grocery shopping telling our children don't touch anything, don't run all over the store and no showing out. By the time, our children reach the teenage years if there is no guidance and no discipline established early in their life, it may be a little too late to start then, our children need to know the difference between the words yes and no, right and wrong, but there is hope.

There is more than one way to cook chicken, fried chicken is not the only way. Therefore, there are so many ways to get our youth back on track. Such as listening to them, learning from them, loving them, helping them, teaching them how to be respectful, reaching them, challenging them, giving them responsibilities, so on and so forth.

Next time anyone thinks on doing something wrong. Think real hard on how it's going to take away and cost you, your future.

Our children are the future, I care!

My Faith and God's Mercy, Grace and Favor

The Lord is truly a Miracle Worker and He never sleeps nor slumber; during my earlier days while stationed at Fort Lewis, Wa. I was trying to make it back to the base on a Sunday evening from Seattle to be ready for duty at 0500, Monday morning.

It was about 10:30 pm, I begin to start feeling fatigued driving on I-5 near the Federal Way area. By the time, I reached McChord Airforce Base the exhausting feeling and the will to get to Fort Lewis, Wa grew stronger and stronger against each other.

15 minutes from reaching the front gate of the base, I fell asleep. Suddenly I was awaken to find myself spinning across all 4 lanes of the freeway. First instinct, I started to straighten out the car and get it under control.

Everything was happening so fast, the more I tried to control the car, the more the car kept spinning. I can recall seeing, an 18 wheeler and a little small compact car in the rear view mirror.

I had stopped trying and yelled out Jesus, three times. Immediately my car stopped close to the middle of the center divider of the freeway facing the direction of the oncoming traffic. I safely pulled over to the side of the road and I started to Praise the Lord for keeping me and for protecting me.

I said to the Lord, Thank you for allowing the 18 wheeler to pass me by. I said Thank you for allowing the little compact car to pass me by. But Lord, when it came to you; you didn't pass me by. Jesus didn't pass me by, that's faith, mercy, favor, grace and my miracle from the Lord.....He didn't pass me by, I still get excited when I think about that night on the freeway in Tacoma, Wa.

Jesus, is our present help in the time of trouble.....anytime, anyplace and any where.

God is Faithful with his Promises:

God told Moses whatever you want me to do, I'll do it. He told Moses whatever you need me to do, I'll do it. God spoke to Moses face to face like a man speaking to his friend, therefore Moses had found grace and favor with the Lord.

Moses trusted God and God trusted Moses to carry out a mission by delivering the children of Israel out of the hands of Pharaoh because he had heard their cry. Isn't it amazing how God spoke to Moses through a pillar of cloud by day and by night. God spoke to Moses through the burning bush and even Moses had to scratch his head and stand in awe because the burning bush was burning and it did not get destroyed.

Moses had his moments, he wasn't able to speak well. But God allowed him to write five books in the Old Testament. Moses had some issues with Pharaoh because Pharaoh wanted to do what he wanted to do and he did not know God. So God had to show Pharaoh who He was and how much control he had over Pharaoh. When God hears your cry, something is getting ready to happen for your good. God has a way of stepping in and taking over.

Moses went to God, and asked God will you show me your Glory? God explains to Moses I'll show you my goodness, I'll show you my grace and I'll show you my mercy. But Moses no one has ever seen me and lived.

From the beginning, God prepared Moses gave him grace and favor. This compelled Moses to have the boldness to not be afraid and to ask God for anything from his heart. God tells Moses, this is what I want you to do for me and I'll show you what I am able to do for you in return. God says, Moses go to a certain place and there will be a rock for you to stand on.

So Moses gets the chance to see God's glory pass from the back of him. God tells Moses while my Glory is passing by, I want you to be on the Clift of the rock and I'm going to cover you with my hand as I pass by. God said I will take away my hand and allow you to see the back parts of me. But my face will not be seen.

Moses was so uplifted, transformed until the skin of his face appearance changed so brightly from God's glory this caused him to wear a veil in order to speak with Aaron and the children of Israel. Moses had enough courage to ask God to do something that has never been done before and God did it just for him.

God fulfilled his promises unto Moses. God will do the same thing for us. Next time we want God to do something for us, don't be afraid to ask him. Instead have enough courage and the faith to believe God can do it and he will for you. Don't be afraid to take up your bed or even make up your own bed and walk. If you feel like leaping after being down for a while, leap. God can take the things that are used up and looking no good and make a change into showing it all good for his glory.

Too often people give up so easily when the works or the blessings doesn't happen right away. What you have to understand is, we have to be prepared to handle the blessings and the works from God. The blessings of God are filled with so much richness of his Glory until the human mankind can't handle it. So, there is going to be some hills to climb, some mountains to reach and it may be a few storms along the way. There may be times when you feel like crying, go ahead and let it out. There may be times when you're going to be faced with something or someone you have lost. There are going to be many days when you gotta fight to keep and hold on to the faith in God. When you find yourself in a very dark place and it leaves you wondering does anyone care? Remember, God is your light to get you out of your dark, dark place.

These things are needed to take place for a lesson in our growth, for guidance, for discipline to sharpen your tools and to build your faith, your trust, your courage in God. When does anyone know how to have faith in God, trust in God and know that God will make a way out of no way unless you encounter some experiences with God. Now God doesn't have any respect of person and he loves us all the same. But, we all have different levels of faith because of our heart.

Our God will take the things that are in secret and use them to reward us openly. He will also bring to pass the things that has never ever been seen or heard before. There is no one here on earth can say, they have seen, heard or even felt in their heart the many blessings that our God has for those who love him.

With his grace and favor my God, your God, our God is able to pay off your home. Leave you with a zero balance with the title in your name and in your hand.

With his grace and favor our God is able to restore the love in our families. Because our families are under attack. With so much brokenness, we are so disconnected and so dysfunctional. Will the fathers and the mothers ask God to work on you and get the love back deep into your soul and in your bones. Too many of our sons and daughters, our young adults have fallen off the side of the road from lack of love, lack of guidance and discipline.

Therefore God has called the old because they know the way. He has called the young because we are strong. All of those who have made it to the top don't forget about the ones who are at the bottom. Without the bottom there is no top, because the bottom is, what holds up the top.

With his grace and favor God is able to make you the owner of your company. Where you are the only one who signs all the checks. Be motivated enough to be one of the best professionals in the community. There is going to be some merits and some demerits happening in our lives, just to show us who we are. We have to continue on making up our minds and get it fixed within our hearts. That we will prevail...

The key criteria is, we all have a story to share, like a tree full of branches all around and covered on each side. There is one tree but so many stories to move and shake up this world to declare, the God that we serve can and will do anything.

After feeling bent out of shape, compressed and stretched in all directions. God is still a true man of his word. He's able to give us the ability to be resilient and to recover from a very difficult change.

We often hear the words! We walk by faith and not by sight. We also have to understand, with the same faith we must show God our works. Without faith, it is impossible to please God and remember he will reward anyone who diligently seeks him.

So along with your faith, keep working on your craft, keep working on your gift and keep working on yourself. Put the work in and put your time in!

Millions into Billions! How could anyone make a dollar with only fifteen pennies in their pocket? With his grace and favor, we have to find a way. Don't let anyone take away your voice to speak, your prize to reach and/or the air we need, to breathe. Keep tapping on the door until you could see yourself getting in.

If and when, we are faithful over a few things. Our God will make us a ruler over plenty of things. He is Faithful with his Promises....

You are created to Win!

What is it about music?
The way it touches the soul like Love.

What is it about music? The way it touches the soul like Love. Allow me to explain my thesis; music is a very unique form of expressions used through the sound of harmony, melody and the lyrics that can reach many levels of one's life. Music brings a reality to allow the listeners to feel, see and hear what the artist is performing.

Music has a brilliant way of displaying art to compel an individual to invest in, grow in and reach every soul across this nation and around the world. Music started way back in the beginning of time as far as anyone can remember.

Music was a strong motivational method used as a tool to get many cultures encountering difficult lifestyles back in the early centuries. When there was nothing else to do, the sound of someone's voice along with some rhythm became a song to remember.

There are so many styles of music such as jazz, hip hop, rhythm and blues, classical, gospel, country, rock and roll, Latin, pop, rap, opera and perhaps a few more to ease your mind.

Music has a way of speaking to your mind, your intellectual capacity of your heart and soul. There is a song for every kind of feeling a person may experience during the first break of dawn.

Music is a gift! Whether you can play an instrument, or sing and play an instrument while singing at the same time. Which ever one is your gift or passion, you are considered among the elite with an incredible gift.

Music gives you an experience towards a life changing moment. The change can cause one to see life completely different and restore the hope, the love and the peace that's missing in our world today. This change can and will definitely heal you and deliver you from the tough emotional scares that's been hanging around like a shadow for years.

The Heaven's are open with all kinds of perfect gifts and good gifts to flow down upon the people in the world. Music will always be a reliable source to bring completeness and to make one whole. Music is used to bring closeness, to bring happiness, to bring forgiveness and to bring openness.

Music is uplifting, reaching, teaching and can make you start to dancing. The tempo can range from being slow, medium, fast and up tempo. The touching and rich sound of music does make folks all around this world dress like there is no tomorrow. It gives a ray of sunshine back into a positive way.

Music during the holiday season does put everyone in a happy, loving and singing mood as we all end the old year and begin to welcome the new year to new beginnings. Music is graced with sounds of joy, peace and excitement during the last few months of the year. It would be very delightful if the sound of music along with love would spread throughout the entire year and not just the holiday season.

On another note, music has made many songs of sadness from breakups, a loss and anything else affiliated with a broken-heart, and simply brokenness. These types of songs have really pushed people in the right direction in life and it allowed one to grow while trying to pull it together from a terrible situation.

Singing a sad song is temporary, it would not be a great ideal to stay in that kind of mood because it's not healthy. It causes depression to overtake you and it will make your life miserable.

Singing a song with the right joyful spirit makes the atmosphere smooth, enjoyable, exciting, inspirational and encouraging. The lyrics that are used in those songs written from a tough experience can help one reach the highest mountain, climb that slippery hill, walk on the water and float around in the air like a butterfly. Some songs can even make one meltdown like butter.

From my own personal perspective music is my life, it's like a love song that means so much and has touch my life in many ways.

Writing a song along with the melody, the tempo, rhythm, lyrics, the beat, the style takes so much practice, practice and more practice to sharpen up your craft.

Anything worth having and worth keeping with your name on it will take some work depending on how bad you want to succeed. But, if this is your passion by all means, follow your heart.

During the process of fulfilling your passion for music or anything else in life will bring some lonely days and with no one around to be found. Then after the hard work is done or the success has finally come is when everyone suddenly appears from all directions of life. Never could understand that concept but it is a part of life.

How good it feels to be touched and moved by some uplifting spiritual songs or some nice romantic songs. When nothing else will work the heartfelt and beautiful sound of music will.

Music has the same effect on life as love does when it touches someone's life. Music can create a love song.

There are decades and decades of songs with a sound of harmony and melody that has a way of touching and revitalizing your heart with a sincere love that will move one in the right direction. Those songs back then and even now demonstrates the true meaning of love. Which does display a polished ending.

Singing a song that brings healing, deliverance is a faithful source of inspiration.

Love takes a person and the world to a completely different level. Love does wonders, love conquers all. Love will clean up and straighten up all the spots and wrinkles that we are experiencing today.

Preface

To keep us all humble! Writing a Book, titled "Life is so Precious"

I received the gift of writing shortly after the passing of my mother 20 years ago. I felt so compelled to write about life to reach every man, every woman, every teenager, little boy and little girl, the hopeless, the homeless, the broken lives dealing with so much hurt and pain, low self esteem individuals and those experiencing deep depression. To reach the unreachable, to touch the untouchable and to speak to the unspeakable, every man and every woman in prison, this is for you too.

A man or a woman that have friends must show themselves to be kind and friendly. It's beginning to feel as though we are losing our own mankind, so I care. Everything I have written, God has given it all to me. Therefore, I am motivated, dedicated, disciplined, driven, selfless and focused to make this happen. To everyone; Don't give up, don't ever give up, no matter what comes and goes in your life. We can't quit, or else you won't win!

The Lord has a reward for all of us, once you have made it to your finish line. Your gift/gifts will make room for you and will bring you before great men, believe this. There is absolutely Nothing Impossible, with God. In fact, all things are Possible to them that believe. Because the Lord, loved me so much I truly love him with my whole heart......He's a loving God full of compassion; He's a Keeping God for His grace and mercy remains forever! Jesus loves you and I, therefore he has proven time after time; Love isn't love, until you have given it away, to comprehend this further, your actions speak louder than your words..

I am writing to share my experiences, my expertise, my wisdom, my knowledge and my ideas just to help somebody else, make it....My desire is to do more and to give back more to the community..

My dream was actually to make it in the NBA prior to joining the United States Army, 26 June 1987. But, to run across and meet The Legendary Magic Johnson, 2001 and play a basketball game against Magic Johnson at the 24

Hour Fitness Center was one of the greatest, greatest moments during my military career. To everyone, Magic still have the game. The two teams were tied at 9 points apiece. Magic did this behind the back over the shoulder pass to his team mate, made the basket and they won the game. Magic was so cool, humble, professional and down to earth to meet, I can handle being around the stars and high profile people. Prior to getting deployed to Iraq, I ran into Magic again, he signed the picture we took together from 2001 and I appreciate that. Thank you Magic

ESPN: You guys played a major role, major part and were a great supporter for everyone in Iraq, I found a secret spot with one of the units in the prison area to get away from the madness and watch the ESPN channel on this big screen television, just to find out about the latest and the greatest of all the sports from the States during the difficult times while recovering from the attacks, this was one of my ways to regroup and try to keep my mind straight and eased to prepare for the next attack. I have watched you guys for years and right now I still have to watch ESPN before going to bed and turning in for the night. I would love to fly down to the Los Angeles, Ca studios and meet everyone and say, you are the best, in person. To the entire ESPN team and crew, thank you!

Throughout my entire military career, my life, the happy stories and the failures. I have taken the mental notes, the passion with a deep love and a concern for others to use as tools to shape this genuine heart to strive for the best in everything I do. Today, I thank God for keeping me, protecting me and for not giving up on me.

Basketball, The Military, The NBA and ESPN along with various church programs and movies has always been a part of my life to see what it's like to be great. My dream is to be in two or three commercials, and I don't care how old I am, I'm going to make this happen. I have this connection that attracts all kinds of people, God has given this to me, it's one of my gifts.

We all have our strengths and weaknesses, and some people may have seen your past, causing them to not see anything good in you. But don't worry, no one has seen your future; but God, he can see the greatness in you.

To all, who have ever experienced losing a family member or a very close friend. You may have even, lost something very dear to you, that has not panned out the way it was planned. Instead, this has caused your feelings to be in a temporary depression phase and has left you spinning the wheels around and going nowhere. This is considered to be a mental disorder that follows everyone around, who have experienced some critical moments along their journey, into being successful human beings.

Magic Johnson and Alton Pete

I have discovered, these type of trying times are setting up your stage to speak in the mic and to share with the world your story, how you've made it over and how you made it through....

So, as we all reflect over our Egypt past, and not to stay there, continue on embracing your present and your future, because this part of your life is brighter than the evening stars, now that's bright.....

"God doesn't look at our age, he looks at our abilities, our heart according to our faith".

Alton Pete at the Barbershop

Just Me!

Paul Millsap and Alton Pete

My Cousin Kia and Alton Pete

Believe in Yourself Again

I understand, that folks every where are experiencing some rough and hard times right now. I would like to start this book out by saying.

Your weeping, may be hitting you up through the night, sometimes the night seems to take for ever to be over. If, you would just hold on, your Joy, your happiness and Joy is coming in the morning. I'm talking about early sun rising, in the morning early.

This is very powerful, because when the sun is rising up early in the morning. The sun is welcoming your new joyous day, by saying good morning, you've made it. Therefore, God has allowed the sun to rule by day, for his glory. It's only doing what God has commanded it to do.

Any witnesses, able to agree, that the Joy of the Lord is our Strength.

"Understand this clearly and precisely: Your life is far worth more than; the silver and gold, the diamonds and the expensive pearl stones, and the black gold oil.....

You are a winner, because it's inside of you"...What you gotta do, what you have to do, is believe in yourself...and believe that the impossible is possible...

There is no greater love, than the love of Jesus Christ. When nothing else will work and there is no one to encourage you and hold you up, His Love is perfect and unending; it will lift you up, again.

Changes are necessary to make and causes one to not stay the same. Just like the time of every four seasons—the fall, winter, spring, and summer. If none of these parts of life took place, our lives would be unfulfilling. In order to appreciate the good times like the bad, one has to change to grow. Have an open mind and open up your heart to accept a change and not say, I'm not going to change. Accept me as I am. Time waits for no one. Don't limit yourself, cutting off your own blessings and missing out on all those golden opportunities. Changes are going to come and changes are going to happen, learn something and make the best of it.

"No one knows, what people had to get through in life to bring them where they are today in their lives. So, when it's your time to shine, go ahead and enjoy your shine". You've earned it and you certainly deserve it!

I have to admit, during the process, during the time God is preparing us. Sometimes you won't understand, sometimes you don't understand. And he has a way of bringing you down to your knees to humble us. But, know this one thing, God holds everything including our future in his hands. He knows, what is best for us.

If, we could remember no weapon that is formed against you shall prosper. Like my mother would say, they can try but it won't work. We are more than conquerors through Jesus Christ. With him on our side, who could harms us and get away with it? No one!

"The Lord is never going to change because he's still the same; yesterday, today and forever more".....

"We are nothing without the Lord, like a ship without a sail on a very windy day, he's the only one who can straighten out your crooked road in a very real way....We owe him everything".

"In the midnight hour, this is the most vulnerable tempting hour of the night when you feel so alone, but God, will give you the Joy and Peace, lift up your hung down head to see your morning".

Be vigilant, watch out for the people who choose to dress like wolf but act like a sheep. Surrounding you, circling around you, hanging out with you by trying to figure out a way, how to get enough information out of you, steal your ideas and then use it to bring you down. They try to play on your weakness, your goodness. They try to play with your kindness, and they do not want you to succeed. Negative people are not worth wasting your time or your energy on. Watch out for the ones, who are like a snake in tall grass. They blend in perfect, but will attack and strike when you are not paying any attention on where and when to take your next step. Your time and your life is so valuable, to you......

Also, watch the seeds that you are planting. If, you are planting the wicked and evil seeds that is what your tree is going to look like which may prevent your favorite fruits from growing on your tree. In other words, what ever it is you are putting out is what you will receive in return. Plant those caring, loving and friendly seeds to allow everyone to enjoy those fresh sweet fruits from your tree, you can't eat all the fruits, it's too many. So share your love....

Good things will happen to good people; just like bad things will happen to bad people. Rich people are always with the rich people; poor people are always left behind. What goes around has to come back around. So, treat people the way you want to be treated because your labor of love is not in vain.

"The spirit of the Lord is so strong and real, that if it was to touch on the back of an elephant, that elephant would move like a cheetah".

Life is just like going out there in the ocean to fish, we have to continue teaching our youth, young adults and sometimes adults how to fish in order to learn something in life and not always catch the fish for them. Give them the chance, the tools and equipment to catch the fish, watch how proud they will become.

***

Watching the news, hearing the people across this great nation moan and groan about when are we going to get a break, get a nice deal, get a hand up instead of a hand turned down. What's in it for our future? Where do we go from here? How am I going to feed my family, take care of my family? Our teachers are not getting paid enough to teach this different generation, why do we see so many homeless people—men, women, and kids—on the street? Taxes are so high—why do we pay so much tax just to receive a small tax in return? We often hear all the time, "We don't have the money or the funds." But everywhere we turn, we see buildings getting built, bridges, bridge toll going up just to cross through to get home safely. Prisons expanding and getting built causing more distance and division within the American family.

I know this may seem impossible, perhaps crazy, to some to even think of this brilliant idea, but this is feasible, possible and we can do it: pay every American family per household in every state a $10,000 grant using the emergency funds that we always send to other countries for natural disasters. Use it for our people. "Charity begins at home; then it spreads abroad."

We are having a natural crisis with our own families here in America. This money will build the economy, put people back on their feet; this absolutely, positively will alleviate, diminish, and minimize the stresses of life that our families are facing every day. This will decrease the crime in various communities. This will give the people a valid reason to live again, to smile again, to hope again.

As prominent and influential leaders, we have to show that we care, and this starts from the top leading down to the bottom. "When you take care of your people, your people will go out of their way to take care of their leaders."

But can't we see? Look around. Our people are hurting so bad, and my heart is for the people of all cultures. I don't care what the color of our skin is—we all bleed the same color, and that color is red. I care!

"Pride, fear, and wavering faith can cause anyone to miss out on the things, promised from God. God is trying to reach you, keep you, and catch you from falling too hard."

"Let's make the Lord glad with our success and not grieve his spirit with our failures."

After all, he is a God of prosperity, and he gives us total victory. A just man or woman may fall a few times, but they always get back up with the right mind.

There is nothing new under the sun. Everything eventually repeats itself. Therefore, you don't have to let your good deeds be evil spoken of. You don't have to let your right hand know what your left hand is doing. Be wise and be more careful in what you do!

"Through prayer, our praying without ceasing has a way of touching the helm of his garment; it'll move him, way up there in Heaven. Whatever good thing you want him to do for you, believe it and it shall be done."

Prayer still works!

"Like David in the book of Psalms, I would have fainted had I not seen the Lord's goodness in this land of the living."

"Out of every bad situation, your good has to come out of it."

Wait for the Lord and be of good courage.

"It's the little things that add up to be much. Make an effort and watch how far you go." Keep striving!

To whom the Lord has blessed, no man and or a woman can curse you.

Keep pressing toward the mark for your prize of the High calling of God in Jesus Christ. God gives us life, so live more abundantly. God is transforming us because the inward man and inward woman are renewed every day. Therefore, we must make better decisions and choices in order to have better leadership and more solutions in the world today to become sufficient qualified role models for our youth and our adults.

Keep in mind, God is more powerful than any force against us. God makes a way when we can't see a way. Isn't it awesome how God can cause the things that do not make sense and the things that are weak to make good sense and make you stronger than ever? God is much greater and bigger than any problem in this world. God has a unique way of taking the heat out of your fire in life, also telling your strong winds and high towering waves to behave, to comfort you by being a lily in your valley as way of returning your happiness.

Isn't it amazing when you finally get there in life, everyone who didn't believe in you start to resurface and reappear in your life like they have always been there for you from the beginning of your troubles and your struggles, the same way Peter in the Bible, prior to denying him, did to Jesus when he stood in the back while watching what was happening to Jesus up front.

For those of you, who still feel like you have something to give back to those who are without, something to say that's positive, you still feel strong in your spirit, mind, heart, body, and soul, you want to see more great changes occur, you're into celebrating when it's someone else's time to shine and won't get jealous because your time is on the way too, secure within yourself, still believe that God is unlimited, the sky is not the limit, because there are higher heights, deeper depths; and he has no respect of person, and you know without a doubt that God is real, who has that kind of power to do anything, everything, and all things. Keep pressing because it is our generation's time to get ours and to make things happen. God sees something great in us when no one else does.

**

Life is full of a whole lot of ups and so many downs: Sometimes life will hit you with a big punch and knock you down. How to persevere and get back up again? Allow me to explain my story.

I believe after getting knocked down, you'll feel strong enough to stand on your feet, square your shoulders, hold your head up high toward the blue sky, and fix in your heart. You will make it, and believe it's going to be ok.

This also depends on how we are raised. Do your loved ones, still believe in you? God has a plan for your life; you will be tested, tried in the fire, in the valley at times, sometimes devastating tragedies leaving you all alone. These things come to build character and get you to the next level. God can put you in a place where you have to trust him and know he's the only one who can bring you out of a difficult situation. People, family, and close friends will leave you; it's part of the process. Do not allow any of this to deter you, to distract you, and/or cause you to fall short. Remember this is for your good. Jesus said he will never leave you or forsake you. He *promised*, there is nothing covered that will not be revealed; neither anything hid that will not be made known.

Being fearful, doubting, feeling some form of rejection, and being angry will cause anyone to lose focus, give up, throw in the towel, and quit. Life has a way of teaching us a few things along the way, so I had to learn to be more discreet and not share with everyone the next move in sight. Some people will not want to see you succeed and exceed, so we have to succeed anyhow, regardless. Some people will not believe in you anymore and any longer. You have to continue on believing in you, for you. Next time when someone tries to whisper something bad in your ear, use it as a form of motivation, shake the dust off your feet, and keep on running.

One exciting thing to know about the Lord: whenever trouble is in your way, when you ask him to send his peace, everything and everybody will be still and come to a halt for you. Life sometimes has the appearance of a newly structured building, the beginning stages does look complex, bleak and empty, out of place, and extremely hard, leaving you wondering, *What have I gotten myself into.* But the finishing product looks organized well put together, perfect, whole, unblemished, brand new, hopeful—just the way God has planned it for your life. You've got to get through the rough part in order to enjoy the good part of your life. God is faithful in his promises; whatever he says, he will do. He is not like a man, who tells you something and gives you his word and then turns around to do something else.

It is always more blessing to give than to always receive; when Jesus walked the earth, he gave and it made a difference and he changed so many lives of the people during that time, especially for those who would travel miles and days, just to get a miracle and have their needs supplied from him. Our churches and also various organizations all across this great nation, has to do more and do much better to see a change and make a difference in the lives of so many people, who are desperately seeking God for a change in their life. Or else, how can one compel or win anyone except they see the Christ in you, the love in you and see your light shining in the midst of a dark, dark world......In so doing, every good thing we all do, will Glorify and touch our Heavenly Father who is high up above.

There is a chronology issue happening with everything going on in the world today; don't let your heart be troubled. There is so much violence in the land because there is not enough love, true love and compassion reaching out to the people. The time is here for those who have always finished last, you will be allowed to come first. God is still answering prayers and what ever it is, you ask him to do, according to your faith, he has all the power to do it......

We all, in this life will have some impossibles occur in our direction. But, we still have to believe, that our impossibles in life, is possible with God.

When those doors are closed and slammed in your face. Be strong enough, to knock that door down and find a way to get through it. Or go around it, to get your dream...your good days, are waiting on you.

So, don't be afraid when your good starts to come in your direction. You've paid your price, embrace your good or else you'll run it all away...it's yours!

You are a Soldier, anything worth keeping will take some hard work and all kinds of work, to hold on to it.....your Faith will be tested, don't let it go.

One of the most loneliness feelings in the world, is when one gives up and quit, because of a few failures....

The most incredible feeling in the world, is watching God unfold and bring to pass those hidden and secret dreams before your very eyes....

Dreams, visions and our thoughts are like the stars that come out at night, there are so many that only God can count them and name them all......He has no limit!

No one, is greater or better than the next person. Everyone has flaws, that God continues to forgive every single day.

As we all, remain focused and driven to reach those prodigious dreams, visions and endeavors. Remember, you've got to keep the faith to see the blue sky above those dark, thick and gloomy clouds....Like a furry caterpillar has to craw along the way. Get transformed or disintegrates into a beautiful work of art to fly around like a butterfly during the day....that furry caterpillar will and is going to change sooner or later, into that beautiful colorful butterfly....the new change or the transformation is incredible!

If, we are going to be the head stop looking like the tail. If, we are going to be in the front stop calling the shots from the back....Don't ever be afraid of who you are!

God is so powerful enough, to calm every storm or defuse any difficult situation; he controls the wind and tells it to stop blowing. He can tell the high waves to come back down. He'll look at the rain and cause it to stop falling from the sky. He still have the power to tell the fire to stop burning and to not consume anyone. And also tell the fog, to keep it clear....

Our God will provide and supply your needs; He got you, he'll make something out of nothing, all for you...God is still, the Great I am!

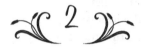

This Is My Story

The passing of both grandparents true and dear to my heart really makes me feel empty until this very day and time of my life. On my mother side of the family, we my 2 brothers, my sister and I were just closer to that side of the family than our father's side.

As a little boy when I got hit by a car at the age of 6, I don't remember the actual accident or the impact that it caused but while in the hospital for over a year with 2 broken legs with a cast up to my waist I remember vividly seeing my grandfather, my grandmother, my father, my mother, uncle Winston, aunt Catherine, uncle Pop, uncle Ervin, aunt Betty, our late church Bishop Albert Lee Jackson, and there were so many others who were there at the hospital every single day. Everyone was praying for me to walk again, so after finally getting home I remember many times walking down the hallway holding on to the walls with the cast up to my waist on both legs. My mom kept telling me to get back in the bed before I crack the cast. She must of forgotten the prayer to see me walk again. God had me getting out the bed nearly everyday to walk, this was Miracle.

***

One very special moment in my young military career, I was able to speak with my grandmother upon returning back to the states after serving over 2 years in Hanua, Germany. I asked her if she make me about 2 or 3 sweet potato pies and she replied of course I'll do that for you.

I made it home safely, went by to see my grandmother and she surprised me with 7 sweet potato pies, felt like Heaven. But, I only had one because my family were helping themselves to the pies while I was busy seeing everyone after getting back in town.

***

When I was very young, my grandfather shared the story about the old man and the little boy with a donkey riding through the town. Every time the old man was riding the donkey through the town, people would be saying, "How could the old man do that to the little boy and make him walk?" Another day would pass, and the little boy would be riding the donkey, and people would say, "How could the little boy do that to the old man and make him walk?"

The point of the story from my grandfather is, you just can't satisfy people and keep them happy.

When we were little kids, my grandmother would pluck our ears every time we would sit next to her after visiting her and my grandfather. Makes me chuckle thinking about it right now. We would say "Grandma," and she would say, "Momma just love you."

My grandfather and my grandmother were the best.

***

Uncle Ervin and Aunt Betty: These two on my mother's side of the family are my favorite, hands down. It's because of my father and my uncle Ervin getting drafted in the army that I felt compelled to join the army and be all I can be. I was inspired by both of them to succeed and exceed to the highest level within both sides of the family. As a little boy, when I didn't even know myself, my uncle Ervin and my aunt Betty would keep me so often until everyone used to think they were my parents. As they said in the earlier years, I favored my uncle Ervin. Now his son—my cousin Kia—and I look alike.

I have so much respect and high praise for my aunt Betty. When my uncle Ervin got drafted for Vietnam in the 1960s, my grandmother, my mother, Aunt Catherine, cousins Queenie and Otha Lee shared the story about how my aunt Betty stuck by the entire family's side throughout the war, awaiting the news regarding my uncle Ervin who went MIA for six months, they were only dating during that time.

Finally, we learned he had been shot in his leg and was transported to Germany then back to the States. I admired my aunt Betty so much, and eventually realized that is exactly the kind of woman I desired to have in my life. Who will be there through thick and thin, all the way until the end. In my entire life. Aunt Betty has always been the same—sweet, very kind, still young-looking, and takes exceptionally good care of my uncle Ervin.

***

Being a PK (Pastor's Kid): That experience was a lot of pressure—all eyes on you, no one there showing you what to do. Church folks looking at every move you make and watching every breath you take—literally being assessed, analyzed, and critiqued all at the same time. I was so young and still learning about life. I would tell anyone to run if you can't handle the heat. But for those of you who are called to be a PK, this will make you stronger to last longer. It does bring power and favor living on the big front stage.

My brothers, my sister, and I handled it well. This part of my life actually prepared me throughout my military career, believe or not. This allowed me to be more aware of my surroundings and to keep doing the right thing and to remember people are watching you when you don't even know it. Sometimes God will wake me up in the middle of the night to write and/or sing a new song. It's amazing how God does that with me, when he wants to get glory from the gift and the gifts he has given to you for free. One has to completely understand that God is and will always be in control of our lives.

Every good gift and every perfect gift comes from above. My gifts were a part of me from the day I was born, manifesting after my mom passed away twenty years ago, and now it's time to share it with the people across this entire world. Our gifts are given to us so we can help someone else instead of keeping it among ourselves. As your plans and your purpose unto God becomes clearer and more understandable, there is no limit to what God can do for you as long as we are giving back to others. When the Lord prayed over the two fish and the five loads of bread, that was for the multitude; but for his disciples, he gave them twelve full baskets left over. What a miracle. So when we give to others in need, we are planting a seed. God will keep his promises and give back to us over and over like an open window from which flows down many blessings from heaven until we will not have enough room to receive it all. God is always looking above and beyond for us to supply our need.

***

Mother Anna Mae Johnson: Mother Johnson, by far to me, was one of the best church mothers a church could have. She was stern, firm, spiritually strong, mentally strong, and she did not play. I used to think she could look through you like a building without walls.

When I finally made it home from Hanau, Germany, everybody was so excited to see me, until I could not get around to speaking to Mother Johnson. So Mother Johnson called my parents every day for nearly two weeks to say, "How come Alton hasn't come by to see me and speak to me?"

My father would mention to me about Mother Johnson calling for me to see her; then my mom would say the same thing. I finally, made it over to where

Mother Johnson sits in her favorite spot in the church, and I could tell she was so happy to see me, because of the way she smiled at me.

On this particular Sunday after Sunday school, she smiled and gave me a hug. She asked me, "What took you so long, boy?"

I said, "Mother, everyone kept pulling me, and I couldn't get through to you."

She said, "Next time, don't let folks do that to you." She also said she prayed for me while I was away in the service (she meant the army, or military, but I'll settle for "the service"), and that touched me. Then she asked, "Did your father and your mother tell you that I called?"

I said, "Yes, ma'am."

She said, "All right, you can go now."

Thank you, Mother Anna Mae Johnson. There is no one like you.

***

Deacon Odell Green: I sincerely appreciate Odell. He was the only one out of the entire church congregation to give me something to take with me on my journey of joining the army, whereas others were too busy crying, being sad, and in shock to learn I was leaving home to become a better man.

Odell pulled me to the side in the church cafeteria and said, "Alton, I see you as one of my sons besides Anthony and Rico. When you get out there around the drill sergeants and away from home, ask God to have favor on you and watch what he will do."

I started to ask God for favor with man the first day I left home on my way to holding station in Oakland, California, to board the airplane to Fort McClellan, Alabama, until this very day God's favor has been over me. Thank you, Deacon Odell Green. You are so missed!

***

Bishop and Mother Donald Murray: You two are incredible. These two called me every month in Iraq, and had the entire Good Samaritan Church family in prayer over me. That's Love!

Bishop and Mother Watson, the entire GloryLand Church family; I will not forget you. Mother Watson, thank you for your love and understanding regarding the passing of my mom.

Bishop Bob Jackson, Bishop Noel Jones and Pastor Joel Osteen: I was able to catch the church services, way over in Iraq because I had an Iraq friend on the FOB (Force Operating Base) install a television disc with over 1,000 channels. Thank you for the strength, the encouraging words, and for being real men of God.

Through my mother's prayers as a child: God raising me up from the death after getting hit by a car at the age of 6, giving me another chance at life.

She told me one day while being home on leave in the Army, that she would give us her last and we didn't even know it. That melted me down like butter. After loosing her, I realized that she was actually the strength for the entire family. I would give her anything without even hesitating. Between her and my dad, she was the one to give me my first twenty dollar bill. We would tease her growing up after coming home from work and getting paid. She always asked, all five of us, where is her money?

I used to wonder, how did she know when everyone got paid and kept track? So, when you keep your hands tight and don't give she said God would put holes in your pocket. Sometimes, I could hear her say, you can't stop the birds from flying over your head, it's too many.

Earlier in my military career, my mom would always remind me to not look for others to encourage me, she said you have to encourage yourself. Each time I was able to call home from Germany, my mom would always answer the call, that's love. On the other hand, my dad would say a few words, then hang up the phone. I could hear my mom saying Eugene you hung up the phone.

When I called back, I asked my mother what happened, she said your daddy hung up the phone. So after while because of the nine hour time difference my mom would start to snore in my ear. During the beginning years of my mom's passing, and seeing her take that last breath on Thursday evening 5 October 1995, I was so troubled in my mind and my heart until I asked God one evening would he and could he amend my heart. That night in a dream, God told me that, not only is he a father to the fatherless but he is God enough to be a mother to the motherless. That blew me away.

***

My father walking away from us during the most critical needed moment ever. Many of times it was unbearable, unbelievable just like a horrible nightmare in a dream, so many days and nights of tossing and toiling, thinking and searching within my heart what to do next, but we made it. To all the Father's out there, when you are proud of your sons and your daughters, you have to continue to show it, so that we may know it. It really doesn't matter how old, we as children become, we need that support and guidance from our fathers. Blood is thicker than mud all day long. When your father and mother forsake you, then the Lord will take you up. Being the oldest is like climbing the highest mountain, walking on water through the depths of the sea and coming out of the lowest parts of a valley.

There were many of days I felt like I didn't know who I was and I felt lost by trying to put my brothers and my sister ahead of me just to keep us close and together as a family. The main thing I decided not to do in my heart, was to walk away from them during the trouble and the struggle, the heat and the fight to make it. With it all being said, giving up on them was not an option, it was my duty as the oldest to be there in any way possible that I could while fulfilling my obligation with the military.

Every day and night, I had to ask God to give me the strength, the courage, the endurance and the unconditional love. Because loosing a mother will change you, it's a different type of life style. Words are very strong and powerful; being told I have a new family, asked so many times; how much time do y'all need to get over your mother, y'all are all grown, you don't need me any more.

These words have made me so strong and only God helps me with the pain every day and at night, some days are better than others.

This is like one of those big fat pills that's hard to swallow, you take the pill with a glass of water, the water goes down first but the big fat pill is stuck in your mouth and then it starts to taste funny because you are trying to decide how and when to swallow the pill, it's funny how that works, quite a disarray.

To not celebrate a milestone, honor, recognize the sacrifice of the Army with 26 years 4 months for the remarkable services of my career from my father is beyond any excuse to be justified how one could ever overlook such an eminent distinguished and noteworthy achievement. After purchasing an amazing brand new home, I celebrate and praise God everyday, instead.

***

The lost of my only sister, April 1st: Until this day, it's still tough for me. One day she wanted me to make some tea cakes for her. It was about 2 dozen, she told me that she ate those things in 3 days, I told her you were being greedy. I learned how to make tea cakes from my grandmother and my aunt Catherine. My sister had a very strong personality with a loving heart, so every now and then I had to remind her, that I'm the oldest. The four of us were so strong, even more so after our mother passed. We became inseparable, connected and stronger continuously.

After loosing Yvette, there were times the feeling of being all alone and feeling like I'm all by myself has creeped into my mind. But God, has given and has restored the peace that I need to ease those terrible thoughts. "There is no such thing of a closure, those wounds remind me many days that they are open when the birthdays come around, special moments come around, Mother's Day is a big day to remember forever. Sometimes, I could see the both of them in my dreams. I thought, I was humble enough after loosing our mom, but since loosing our only sister makes me more and more humble, every single day.

"To all the mothers, grandmothers, sisters, aunts, God-mothers, female cousins, female friends, you guys are the best. There is none like you! I'm not leaving the men out, but our women has the super glue of love to keep the family together, they are so strong and we need them. Truth be told, I believe our women should get paid the same salary as men on all levels. After all, in my opinion, this is a man and a woman's world....Women know how to pick up the pieces and keep it going, men are always dropping the pieces and walking away.

***

Leon Pete and Pastor Phillip Pete: These two brothers of mine make me very, very proud of their endeavors and their terrific achievements. Leon has kept me motivated in the education area of my life, to keep pushing for the master's, then the PhD. Because he graduated from San Francisco State University and persevered in spite of everything we lost, he didn't give up.

Pastor Phillip Pete, on the other hand, is the preacher in the family. Reminds me so much of my dad with that burning fire shut up in my bones and that anointing to destroy the yokes. I stand in awe and not envy, by all means, of his marriage to one lady for twenty-four years. This is remarkable, and what a great example to follow, which has given me the hope to get the same thing for my life. I could see the growth, the strength, the courage, the faith in both of them. The three of us is all we have, and we have plans on making it, like our mother used to say. We are going to make it, mark my word.

***

The loss of my cousin Raymond: He was a sensational rapper—so good I wanted him to say a piece on one of our songs on the album my brothers and I are planning on recording. I received a call from my cousin three months prior to him getting shot. He was reaching out, and we failed him. Family is critical and so much needed in the world today. There is a strong disconnect that I feel led to help mend the broken pieces back together again. When my grandmother was alive, we were closer and stronger than today. I feel as though somewhere we have lost the score. Thank God for my uncle Ervin and my aunt Betty, I see the hope. Family always will come first.

We have to figure out a way to bring the immediate family back together by having dinner with everyone present at least a few days out of a 7 day week; Sunday being the most important, because it's a soul food family day for everyone to gather and socialize.

I have this very strong vigorous determination along with compassion to encourage every family to come back home. There are so many prodigal sons and daughters, lost in the wilderness without anyone showing that they care.

***

My favorite and only niece Seraya (I call her Sheraya), Lucy and Peggy: my niece gravitated to me shortly after my mom passed at the age of 3. I couldn't leave my niece's sight she wanted to go every where I went, some folks always thought that she was my daughter. She was around 4 we had dinner at my place I told her she could go in the bathroom to wash her hands, about 20 minutes later we were waiting on her to finish I knocked on the door to see if she was ok, I noticed the entire bottle of hand washing soap was empty, she said uncle you told me to wash my hands and I was trying to wash them clean, I said Sheraya I didn't mean to use up the whole bottle. I remember Sheraya had turned 6 or 7 so I surprised her with a fifty dollar bill for her birthday. A few days later I met with my family for dinner, Sheraya and I went to the grocery store for a couple of items. She saw something that she just had to have, I said go ahead and get it. We were waiting to check out and after I purchased the items I asked Sheraya did you really need that toy, I gave you some money for your birthday, she said I know uncle but you didn't give me a gift. I was surrounded by some ladies and they laughed, I chuckled too. My niece has grown up to be a very intelligent, educated and brilliant young lady at 23, she has her degree from Grambling University and pursuing her major in law; now Lucy and Peggy, these two young ladies are phenomenal, the encouragement, the love, the words of advice, the countless times we all had dinner when I was in town, many times we would dinner and we would have so much fun. When I get married one day, these two ladies have to be a part of this glorious moment. They stepped in and stepped up over 20 years ago, when many times I felt lost, confused, heavy with pain on my chest and hurting from my mother and sister, they were there and they didn't even know it. I sincerely appreciate Lucy and Peggy!

My Uncle Ervin, Aunt Betty and Alton Pete

Alton, Leon, Yvette, Phillip, Sister-in-Law Rehema and my niece Seraya
21 years ago

Odell Green and My Mother

My Mother - The Late Mother Lillian Pete, The Queen of the Pete Family.

❦ 3 ❦

My Military Career

My military career: 26 years 4 months in the Army, 18 month tour in Iraq OIF (Operation Iraqi Freedom). It was a 24 hour flight going over to Kuwait. The first day on the ground we experienced the first mortar attack, I knew then that the heat was on, I saw the scary stare and fear in the eyes of some soldiers, so I walked away because I did not want that fear to rub off over me. From that day until our last day in Iraq, we were attacked every month 6-7 times a month. The loud blast sounds from the IED's blowing up outside the FOB (Force Operating Base), The Mortar round attacks came landing in front of us so many times until it was too fast for any of us to react, the fire fights from this Iraqi apartment building sitting across the street from the FOB, the detainees trying to escape every chance they had, the sandstorm turning the sky completely orange, the heat reaching 147 degrees for six months from May 1st through the end of October and causing the heat index to reach as high as 199 degrees with the full battle rattle on. At night, the temperature would be 103, 104, 105 with humidity. Now, that's hot!

Being out on those convoys, while traveling on the most death trap Iraqi roads in combat, not knowing when or where the next IED, VBIED, RPG, or the Fire Fight attack would occur. We were cautiously aware of the mysterious wire hanging loosely from the overhead bridges and the games of using dead or live animal carcasses to blow us up from a hidden ambush. It was truthfully the Amazing Grace of God protecting us, guiding us, leading us, directing us safely to the next FOB such as: Camp Liberty, Camp Victory, Camp Stryker, Camp Balad, Abu Ghraib, and the largest FOB Camp Anaconda. It didn't matter, how fatigued we all were, outside the wire from the FOB on a convoy, we were fully engaged, alert and ready to defend each other.

Riding on the bird (the Black Hawk Helicopter) was very intense. The guys were locked and loaded with the 50 caliber, the 240B and ready to go. The pilot kept doing these sudden turns, dips and it was causing me to feel so dizzy, sick to my stomach. But, I held on, this is how and why we train; to be the strong, to be brave and to be a soldier.

Seeing the fancy castles with those huge crystal clear chandeliers hanging down from the ceilings, walking on the marble floors, up and down the balconies, and discovering the many fancy sinks and seeing those golden toilets made everyone feel like Richie Rich. The castles were so big, long, wide and so high, you could hear the sounds of the soldiers echoing throughout the castle.

On the outside and around the castle at Camp Victory, there was one of most gorgeous lakes, I have ever seen. Everything looked so clean and pure. Camp Anaconda and Camp Balad had swimming pools, theaters to see movies. I took the bus to view these areas after our unit relocated to Camp Cropper. I don't remember where, but I saw this unique area that looked like the Flintstones. The castle was breathtaking. That bus ride was cautious and everyone on board was very quiet. We had to be ready for the sound of an attack and be ready to react swiftly. We noticed, the bus driver (a civilian lady) was kind of whispering as she gave us the history about certain areas of Camp Victory and the other FOB's (Force Operating Base) near by.

We made history, to be that close and to walk on the grounds of the City of Babylon. Where King Nebuchadnezzar ruled for so many years and with all that history in the bible was made a believer by God, that God is the only one who can walk through a burning fiery furnace with you and not get burned; among the many other miracles seen while he was a ruler.

There was an Iraqi man on the speaker outside the FOB (Force Operating Base) every Sunday speaking for 6 hours, we all knew it was Sunday and that day came extremely fast, nerve racking. When it rain, the mud piles up like snow up to the knees. The 18 wheeler generators running 24 hours a day to provide our power. All of this has deeply affected my sleeping and night of rest, since returning back home to the states. Because the attacks were happening at various times of the morning, during the day, the evening, the late night and the early mornings. I was faced with the questions from many, after returning from that dangerous combat tour in Iraq.

"Were you scared?"

"Were you terrified, afraid?"

"What was it like?"

Fear will come because it's natural when regarding the safety of your life. But everyday and every night I stayed in constant prayer with the Lord to never give me the spirit of fear and He did that just for me. Matter of fact, I was asked by the soldiers to start a prayer gathering at noon everyday because so many were scared to death. I was so honored and so touched to see the heads of all the ethnic backgrounds bowing unto the mighty hands of the Lord while I was able to share the powerful words of prayer with my colleagues. There were so many times during and after the prayer when we kept coming under attack by the Iraqis. But God kept us safe and protected, and he remained that tall fence all around us. We didn't lose not one soldier.

Just to show, how good God is, there were times we were outside the building chopping it up and happy to see each other because of the crazy hours everyone were putting in; a mortar round would hit the wall right in front of us. The mortar round would not and did not explode. Only God!

When the time came for us to leave Iraq and the tour was coming to an end, we were able to embellish so many heroic deeds for the Iraqis. I was so exhausted beyond measure on that bus ride to the airport to fly on the C130 back to Kuwait to wait a few days to board that huge commercial Quest flight to Ireland and then finally back to the United States—our land of the free and home of the brave.

I haven't had McDonalds in so long until, while waiting those few days in Kuwait, I had 5 hamburgers and 2 large orders of French fries. Anyone been deployed, you understand!

The flight was twenty-four hours. I slept and woke up so many times to discover we were still in the air. The anticipation of getting back to the states grew stronger and stronger. Finally, we landed in Maine; and to see some former war veterans welcoming us home at two in the early morning was a feeling that is indescribable. It felt so different, strange, clean, and new.

On the spiritual side, Iraq is the city of Babylon. This was where it all began. Daniel in the Lion's den, and because he continued to pray three times a day, God allowed the lions to be his best friend, where no harm was bestowed upon him. The three Hebrew boys facing the fiery furnace heated seven times than normal telling the king that the God we serve may not deliver us, but we know without a doubt he is able; and as a result, the three Hebrew boys went through the fiery furnace and saw the Son of the Living God with them in the midst and came out without any burns to their bodies and clothes. What a miracle. Close to the Red Sea where God told Moses to stretch out his rod and the Red Sea was divided in half to allow the children of Israel to pass through freely.

Nearby, Paul was going to Damascus to persecute God's people but ended up losing his sight and went on a brand-new mission instead. Jonah making it to the land of Nineveh to preach the gospel to the wicked man. God said if they didn't repent in forty days, he would send a curse on their wicked ways. So Jonah decided which way he would go. He boarded a ship that went deep down below. Jonah told the men, "All this trouble is on account of me. Throw me overboard and watch the ship go free." While reading the Bible all of these years, to be near where Jesus walked through the entire Syria region. In the New Testament, Joseph was told by an angel to flee to Egypt for a short while until Herod the King was no longer around to destroy baby Jesus. These are all my favorite stories and more. Because of the time difference in Iraq, I could completely understand when David declared to praise the Lord to the rising of the sun and to the going down the same. While everyone was praising and lifting up the name of Lord during the day here in the States, it was nighttime in Iraq. I was then seeking more of the Lord at the same time during the night patrolling for our safety.

***

Wearing the army uniform: This part speaks high volume on many levels. I felt so honored to wear the army uniform with all the awards I earned. It is astonishing and astounding, brave, rewarding, fearless, intimidating, a strong feeling of confidence, self-assurance, and more. Many times, I felt like a celebrity. It didn't matter where I went or where I was; people would ease their way over to me to touch the uniform, touch me, ask a whole bunch of questions, walk by me, and smile; and then others have stopped to say thank you. One time on my way home, I stopped at a grocery store to get some fruits, the older lady came over to tell me and said she feels safe being in America. While in Iraq, it was so dusty and dirty over there. I went through so many bags of baby wipes to use over my freshly washed uniforms to keep clean. Wearing the army uniform was my pride and joy; it just felt and looked powerful. I felt some sense of security myself.

***

Photos from Iraq and Combat

$\approx$ 4 $\gg$

The Germany Story

Germany was an incredible breath taking country to ever visit. First time being so far away from home. I actually learned to speak the language and took strong interest in the culture. Had I not joined the Army, I wouldn't ever seen any parts of Germany or Europe. Castles made up with gold, lighting up the evening far in a distance. Never will I forget the time it snowed for a week straight 24 hours a day, what a site to see, the temperature was 15 below zero, so cold your head would literally start hurting. On the autobahn (the freeway, highway) there is no speed limit, you can drive as fast as you want and not get a ticket. While I was stationed in Germany, you never heard much about anyone having an accident driving on the autobahn reaching top speed in their vehicles. Germany is a very clean, clean beautiful country, the restaurants and the food was outstanding. First time ever repelling from that high rocky cliff, what a way to overcome fear build up confidence and courage. Looking down that cliff before my turn came to put on the harness and feeling scared to death, I didn't tell anyone. My chest was beating so hard, I could have started a music band with it, all I needed was some back up singers.

Germany is filled with so much positive energy, happy emotions and strength; the German culture is so strong and wealthy. There is always something to do and learn while enjoying the sight of this epic historical and traditional country. This country by far, was one of the best educational lessons to embrace with richness and glow.

I was able to explore and drive to visit many of the exciting cities such as: Berlin and the wall, where the East and West Germans were divided for so many years. I can recall seeing some of the Germans sitting and standing on the pieces of the wall after the wall was knocked down.

I traveled of course to the popular city Frankfurt and other groups of cities throughout Germany that charmed my interest like Munick, Hamburg, Cologne, Wurzburg, Austria, Bad Kissingen, Baumholder, Bremerhaven, Darmstadt Freisbach, Freudenberg Grafenwohr, Kaiserslautern (K Town), Neuberg, Offenbach am Main, Reinstadt, Reinheim, Ramstein-Miesenbach and Weisbaden,it was quite an adventure.

I do, deeply regret not visiting Spain, Paris, Italy, Heidelberg and Switzerland.

To see where the BMW's, the Porsche, the Audi's, the Mercedes-Benz and the other fast speeding cars were made did appear to be fascinating and enchanting to me. Especially, when the taxi drivers used these vehicles to drive you around in.

Germany is well known for the German/American festivals and the famous Okotberfest festival. In the beginning of my days in Germany, I ordered one of those huge bratwurst sausages at the German/American fest and the German guy gave me a sourdough roll with it, I asked a for a hot dog bun and later found out this is how you eat the bratwurst sausage with the roll. That part was all new to me, still learning. Sunday was the day of rest, everything is closed on Sunday. This was my favorite place overseas to live, take interest in the culture and loved.

I vividly remember, there was a German old lady close in age to my grandmother, who worked on the Hanua, Wolfgang Kaserne for the government. This old lady was very mean, I would speak to her and be respectful towards our elderly every time I would see her. So, one day she surprised me by baking a pound cake, she said we don't call this cake that, here in Germany it's called the Sandkuchen.

Since German people are some of the best cooks, dessert bakers and strong culture people in the world. This Sandkuchen cake was really good, the German old lady had a great heart after all. She started to treat me like a grandson by bringing some sweet pastry treats like some apple strudel, berry fruit tarts, Pflaumenstreusel vom Blech(which was very good) and sour dough bread to the area where we were on detail guarding the Kaserne. Prior, to coming back to the states out of Germany, I was able to see and meet some Yugoslavians and some Czechoslovakians who were living on the Kasernes that we were leaving for the Germans to occupy, it was brief, but the experience was something new to learn about the history of other cultures across the world.

To all the friendly German people, Danke und Tschuss.

5

How to Trust God

Continue to trust in God, without him we are nothing. I had to learn to surrender everything back to the Lord. My heart, soul, body, all of me, humble myself, cry out to the Lord. He does feel our pain, our hurt, hear our cries, he knows exactly what to do.

Faith does come, by hearing the word of God, reading the bible and asking God to fix my life again has worked out perfect for me. Continue to hold on and keep the Faith and remember that God has all the unlimited Power to do whatever we ask him to do.

Someone said to me, "Alton, If God did not think you could bear it, he wouldn't of placed all of these tough moments along your way. Now I agree , we are stronger than we think we are according to God because of the heart and our faith.

> If the sun keeps on shining
> The rain doesn't come
> And if the wind wouldn't and didn't blow in our lives
> You'll never grow.....
> Whenever, there's a rainbow, as beautiful as it looks,
> there will be some rain.

I have yet to see any man or any woman who love to climb mountains. Start to climb up to the mountain top and along the way didn't experience a few slips, falls, close calls and close moments. There will be challenges, no matter what we do in this life.

There is always more than one way to get things done, in other words there is no limit in how far in life anyone could go and become. One monkey does not stop the show. When something or someone peaks your interest, go for it and get it.

I'm just like that Alaskan crab in a bucket with the spikes on my back. Telling people, you better hold on because it ain't no coming back down.... we need to learn how to settle more for greatness over the shortness and stop missing out on all those golden opportunities. Isn't it amazing how nowadays there are yet a few people who try so hard to see you fall down after you have tried so hard to rise to the top. We have to use some common sense and not give anyone a reason to see you fall and dig deep within your heart to understand what got you there in the first place and be wise enough to keep it moving and keep it going.

We have to stay two steps ahead of every situation and utilize discipline. There are those who see you different because you are different, getting to the top is hard, but very easy to come back down. When someone despise you, show signs of doubting you, let that inspire you to make your ambitions. When God gives you a dream, the dream is for your instructions to direct your life. Therefore, no one will understand because God gave you the dream. By way of a deep sleep, a dream or a vision is the only way God will reach us to fulfill our goals. Go out and make it happen, or else a dream is just a dream. We can do all things through Christ that strengthens us.

God has a way of replacing, replenishing, renewing and restoring everything we need in our lives. Our health, our dreams, our goals. We walk by faith and not by sight. The spirit of the Lord searches the deep the things of God. God is The King of Glory, the Lord strong and mighty, the Lord mighty in battle.

Sometimes in reaching our goals, we either have it rough in the beginning and see it easy to the finish line, or we either have it easy in the beginning and see it tougher at the finish line, and or have it rougher from the beginning and tougher to the ending of your finish line. No one really understands why life serves the hand this way. I will say to much is given to much is required based upon your faith. Everyone has some degree of faith! Keep the Faith.

❧ 6 ❧

The Woman Comes First;
She Is the Man's Queen

The importance of treating our women right: Ladies get humbled, loose the attitude, it doesn't make you less than a woman. The woman is the Queen, so women return back to teaching our little girls on how to grow up to be brilliant classy and respectful young ladies. The woman is one of the vital pieces of the man's life. Fellas, women desire and are to be respected, to be cherished, to be adored, seek security, protection, to feel safe, to be loved. Seeks a spiritual foundation, must feel financially secured and must be naturally balanced. Women want a man with a sincere heart and to be in a peaceful place with the right man. We as men must receive our guidance from God on how to keep our women happy/happier. The connection between the two must be deeply rooted, after all the woman is the man's glory.

One of the main reasons why there is such a strong disconnect between the man and the woman, no one appears to remember their role in the friendship and the relationship. People are afraid to ask those honest questions regarding the values, morals, the careers and the future. When it begins to get serious, ladies ask those questions about the medical, dental and vision benefits. Ask those honest questions regarding the financial support for a family without sounding like you are the richest person in the world. Don't forget to ask the questions about the commitment and the exclusiveness connection when it's only you two dating for over 6 months.

Don't assume ladies ask those valuable questions before you get too deep to climb out, that way it won't leave you stuck and leave you bitter. Know your role and don't go with the flow, follow your heart and soul. You'll know when

---

to bring your high walls of Jericho down. Do not expect the man to do it all and know it all, or else you will burn that man out and chase away your good. It takes two to tangle, bring something to the table and not show up empty handed your beauty alone is not enough because overtime beauty fades.

Men are tough, but we have feelings too. I would love to have someone who adds value to my life because I'm willing to do the same for her, or what's the point? Men desire to have that unconditional love with someone special that will cause her to gently float around like a butterfly and touch his heart. A woman has to continue being the woman God has created her to be—strong, virtuous, touchable, unmovable, lovable, full of class, beautiful, phenomenal, extraordinary, uplifting, seasoned, experienced, confident, driven, pursuers, gentle, firm, sweet.

No one could ever take the place of the woman. Her love is powerful; the trust is inevitable. It takes respect to get respect; we men should not stop opening doors for our women. Don't let her walk on the side of traffic. We have to protect and keep our women safe and protected. Women are very emotional people; that's the way God made them. So to all the men, we have to tighten up our shot groups, be flexible, and support their needs. This will potentially lead into healthy and stronger relationships. Our women are like layers of a sweet onion; each time around they become better and better to love, like a honeycomb sweeter for our taste, like fresh fruits and vegetables so good to look at, even from a distance.

Women, when you see that man for you, it'll be just like that Bentley. Once you sit in the front seat and look around at everything you have and want, you will know it. Lastly, women do not bring up any past relationships or ex's in that man's face or his presence. Respectfully and truthfully, a man never wants to hear that, at all.

***

The secret of a successful man: Get humble, lose the attitude; it doesn't make you less of a man. Remember, we are made and chosen by God to be leaders, providers, protectors, the king, so, men return back to teaching our little boys on how to become strong, respected, intelligent young men. Therefore, our role is crucial and vital. Men are required to set the example and lead by example at all times. The head of every man and every woman is God. The head of the woman is the man; we are a reflection of our Lord Jesus Christ. As men, we are stronger physically; that's the way God made us. This is never to be confused with abusing any woman and causing her to be fearful and to be afraid of us in that way. In fact, we have to love our wife as Christ gave himself for the church. Now, that's a lot of love, because Jesus died on the cross for us. A man, unless crippled, lame, or mentally challenged should never expect the woman to pay his bills, feed him, buy him clothes, and have her working while he is chilling at home. It will never make you less than a man to love, to cherish, to adore, to honor, to hold, to cuddle, to kiss, or to shop for the woman you are in love with.

In fact, truth be told, this allows you to be the leader you are called to be; and as you demonstrate that unconditional love, it will translate that giddy love to the woman's heart. Men, learn how to communicate better, ask those valuable questions next time you start to date someone and begin to accumulate some feelings. Questions like, Do you see yourself with this lady in your life? Can you bring her around your family after you have dated for three to six months? Are you willing to invest your time, your love, ready to spoil her, marry her, be with one lady only? Are you willing to support, protect, and provide for her? Do not just assume she knows it all and can do it all. Women work better as a team instead of trying to do it all on their own. Men should never talk down to the woman or disrespect her in a public area. Once the trust is gone, your love alone cannot bring it back. If you ever get mad at your woman, walk away, take a deep breath, let the air out. Stay calm, regroup, get yourself together, and communicate with her. After all, we are to do those things that are pleasing in the sight of the Lord. Keep him smiling and stay pleased with our decisions.

One thing I have noticed in our world and culture today is that the men are not men enough to keep the family together. I appreciate my dad for being there all the way until my mother was no longer around. Honestly, you need the father and the mother to make a strong, healthy family. Everything appears to be out of order because of the man. It is imperative that we be the men that God has called us to be. As men, we can't buy any woman's love because she's priceless. We can show it in more ways than one. Men, we are made to be strong like an ox with the heart of a male lion; if we were to ever fall down to our knees, while down on our knees, we have to think of a way and feel within our heart a way of getting back up on our feet just to fight for life again.

When you find that woman for you, it'll be just like that brand-new home after looking around the outside of the home and then taking that first step through the front door. You will know it. Lastly, men do not bring up any past relationships or ex's in that woman's face or her presence. Honestly and respectfully, women do not want to hear that, at all.

7

Going the Distance

The finish line looks, so small from the distance. After while, once approaching the finish line, your dreams, your goals, look much bigger than the distance. Fruits are always the sweetest at the top of the tree. Much harder to reach than the bottom of the tree. Keep reaching for the top of everything for your life.

In order to move forward, we got to, we have to leave the negativity behind. We must lay it aside and shake off the doubt, continue to shake off the negativity. Because it will weigh you down like rain and dirt turned into mud, that could get heavy. You've got to lay aside every weight and run with patience the race that is set before you.

We have to continue on learning how to go from good to great, great to greater. Because the One up above is the Greatest and he only wants the best from his great.

I'm just a regular person with passion, hope, and with a purpose from my dreams.

God has some surprises for you. Wait on him and Rejoice. They're coming out of the ordinary, unexpectedly, incredibly, extremely, and in an unusually way. There are brighter days and peaceful nights coming your way. There are yet, things hidden that God has to unhide for us with our name on it. Sometimes disappointments and setbacks will propel us to become successful.

We all have to step up to be who we are called to be. We have the potential to be the best and to be great with Christ Jesus on our side. Remember, Faith is and will be at times uncomfortable; a few examples to read about are the three Hebrew boys, Daniel in the lion's den, David up against the giant, Peter in prison, Jonah on the ship, Jesus saying that I am, just to name a few. Anything different will be uneasy, but we will continue to grow from the experience. Faith without works is dead alone, we have to show God what we want and what we can do. He knows. Then we must have the faith and believe we can get it and it shall be ours.

God desires the best for every one of us. He has no respect of person. He is amazing, marvelous, magnificent, extraordinary. There are plenty of examples in the Bible where and when God uses the young and the old to bless. Therefore, there is no excuse to not make our dreams happen. I don't care what anyone whispers in your ear. Keep looking forward. Don't look to the left, don't look to the right. These things deter and distract us and make us afraid to keep moving forward. Look towards the hills for your help; that help comes from the Lord.

Stay focused, keep dreaming, keep exceeding, keep reaching, keep pressing toward the mark for your prize of the High calling of God in Jesus Christ. Continue to speak things into existence. (It works.) Whatever your heart desires, don't you know God hears you, God feels you? Don't stop, persevere, succeed, achieve, stay creative. God wants to hear a good report from us. Every man and every woman should know what their purpose in life is. We have gained so much in this world. Now we have to give back to someone else in need. Dreams are important; they come to give us guidance and tap into our present and future. We have to go out and make it happen, not to let them slip by. Giving God the good news and the glad tidings report!

8

Working Out, Staying in Shape, and Eating Healthy

I could never elaborate on this issue enough. I lost my mom due to diabetes. It is extremely essential to love your body like never before. Working out and staying in shape fuels the body with so much needed energy that helps us to deal with every day's life and all that comes with it. Eating healthy keeps all those main organs fresh and working properly. When you are taking care of yourself your healthy heart will appreciate you. Throughout the year, eat some fruits, vegetables along with drinking plenty of water is key. These things work, only if you use it. Serve your body with plenty of fiber, baked meats, and if you can help it stay away from the fried foods, greasy foods and the fast foods, because they are very very high in fats and will cause high blood, high cholesterol and other health risk concerns. . Ride a bike, go for a hike, take a walk in the park feel that clean air and breeze, visit the gym for a 30-60 minute exercising routine and socializing interactions with other people has a positive way of making one feel brand new. Play a game of golf, try out the bowling league, take a drive along the coastline, attend some sporting events and go see your favorite baseball, basketball or football team. Any type of safe outdoor activities will cause one to feel young again and look young. There is so much left to experience in your life. Stay motivated and be dedicated.

What drives me? I am humble, confident and strong: I have this yearning desire to continue what my mom started and left off by way of giving back, putting a smile on the inside of everyone's heart. Making a difference in the church, the community, in people lives. We lost her at the early age of forty-eight—that's way too soon but God knows and loves her more. My mom wanted the best for all four of us- Myself, Leon, Yvette and Phillip, oh yea Barbara Ann too, my cousin we took in when I was around 11 or 12. Being the oldest both my dad and mom would push me in those days because I needed it, plus I didn't want to disappoint them. We were teased and bullied as kids because my parents made us attend church nearly everyday and those terrible guys would chase us in the house while some of the other kids would hit me long enough before I could get through the door. There were times the door was locked and the guys were hitting me so hard until I could feel the pain in my arm race across my body. After my freshman year in high school I made up in my mind that I wasn't going to run any more, so the entire summer everyday I would do push-ups, my mom kept telling me it was making my chest too big, I said exactly because I was not going to run again, it worked. Never had the fear to run from bullies that day and further more. My sophomore year I was ready for anyone who challenged me, didn't matter how big they were. I would refuse to run just to protect my brothers, my sister and I.

9

Politics and Being Correct

With all respect and all fairness, it's about doing the right thing and making things happen. Upholding the standards and leading by example. I strongly feel as Congress receives the same salary after retirement or term, our military forces should be allowed to receive the hazard pay or the combat pay after returning from Operation Iraqi Freedom (OIF) and OEF (Operation Enduring Freedom) for the rest of their lives. Everyone is so done with this separation and cliques. I am so torn over the lives of our wounded, KIA, MIA, and all those who have sacrificed their lives for the USA. It's all about the importance of the health and welfare of every service member. When I was in Iraq, I can recall vividly the Iraqi men receiving some compensation after getting released from the prison. I wonder why we as Americans do not do the same for our prisoners when they are released to get back out in society to survive. Just a valid point to address this issue in a better compassionate way.

Truth be told, we were the ones on the ground patrolling, policing, fighting in harm's way for our safety, and for the civilians close by in the vicinity. Upon returning home, I have witnessed so many of our servicemen and servicewomen just literally destroyed both mentally and physically. It rips my heart apart into pieces. Coping with the PTSD, the constant nightmares waking up in the middle of the night wondering if I am in Iraq or home safely in America or anticipating the next attack from the Iraqis. Dealing with the vertigo, the repeated headaches and migraines every month since returning from theater. I have so much pain from the surgeries until I'm always asking God to ease and take away the pain.

Since my retirement from the army in 2014 and making it back to the Bay Area, crime has escalated to degrees that are imaginable. For our nation and the state of California being one of the best states to live. We have to do better. No one can really go anywhere without people on the streets holding their hand out for some type of help. That could be at the grocery store, Popeye's and McDonald's restaurant, the gas station, church, the post office, Lowes and Home Depot or anywhere. People on the streets are desperately crying out for help and so many of us are turning the deaf ear and the blind eye. So in way, you have to do whatever it takes to survive. Education is the answer but not the only answer, after we get those degrees we still have to earn enough income to survive. We seem to have lost the heart felt love and the spirit of compassion, "allow the brotherly and the sisterly love to continue".

"On a side note, start on a plan to repair your credit score by working out those issues into preparing to purchase your first new home or purchase another home if, you lost a home in the past". This is an incredible way and the best way to invest, to pay a mortgage and leave those rent days behind. However, I concur and understand we have to do what we can, but don't stay there, don't limit yourself. We have enough land in America for everyone to be a home owner, so do not get caught up and become complacent".

As for me, I am a leader in the front and not calling the shots in the rear. I have visit many in the streets of Richmond, Berkeley, Oakland and San Francisco to look after the homeless and the less fortunate. There was a time I would give some money, now I purchase the food, give blankets and sometimes sleeping pj's to place a smile in someone's heart.

From my perspective and I'm only thinking it, but where are the Politicians? Does anyone care anymore? This is still a reflection of every one holding a political position in our state, city and the community. I often hear the politicians talk about it, no changes as of yet. Jesus mentioned to be a doer of your word. Or else you're just deceiving your own self.

My healthy advice to all the politicians, treat people how you and your family deserve to be treated. We all bleed the same color, excuses are for losers. Don't say what you are not able or willing to commit to. Always mean what you say, people will hold you to that when you may forget. The same rough areas that you walk to get a vote, go and make the same walk in those rough areas after getting elected, it truly shows the people that you care. Be honest, demonstrate and display great integrity along with accountability. The truth supersedes a lie by a long shot. There is still time for change and forgiveness, judgement is drawing closer everyday. When anyone speak false hope to the people, you loose the people. When you be truthful with the people, you gain them. It only takes one match to start a fire, not the whole book.

If, we could waste billions of dollars on the Iraqi people, what about our own people here in America? Minimum wage should be $20.00 or more an hour, there is no way any family can survive in America let alone to purchase a home or pay rent in these expensive apartments. We have so many broken-spirited, hopeless, and discouraged people more than ever. People setting up tents underneath the freeways, BART trails, and public parks like animals in the wild. I was speaking to a homeless lady in Berkeley one Saturday afternoon near the Berkeley University Cal campus. I saw her eating some cat food out of a can she told me that was all she had. This took my breath away. I went to the grocery store to purchase some food for her to last for a week. This made her day. I saw her weeping, and I told her, "You're going be all right." I gave her twenty dollars, and then I drove away.

10

Words of Encouragement

Words of encouragement: I have been approached by so many people saying Alton why are you so strong? My reply is that I have never given up on God and he has never given up on me. Now, I've been through my share of the bumps, bruises, scars, storms and rain, sicknesses and in pain, hills to climb and a valley to walk out of, tragedies too. With the pain, God has made a way of escape to receive my gain. When God gives us enough strength to get back on our feet to run out of Egypt, keep running. There is no need to go back into Egypt for anything. Not for the negative people, poison relationships, mistreatments on the job, disappointments, failures, self pity, low self esteem, some of your so called friends who aren't around to be found, the things that are weighing you down, absolutely nothing. We have to be like Lot from the bible and don't look back. What people don't understand is God will make things go so crazy, stir up your gift and make things so uncomfortable just to get you to the next journey in your life. We have to remember He controls our going out and our coming back in. We don't need to keep bumping our heads in the same spot to realize that hurts. Learn from the first bump around and grow from there. Going back and forth into Egypt for your help only causes one to be deterred. Instead, be prepared and feel renewed to be strong enough from the help of God to not look back, this is very encouraging. Pursue your goals, pursue your ambitions, pursue your endeavors, pursue your dreams, pursue your destiny. Don't give up, don't give in, don't quit, because you will win only if you hold on!

"Like a triangle shape, bigger at the bottom and smaller at top. Not everyone can handle being on top is the reason why so many are at the bottom. Only a few, will get to the top because the bottom is not their final destination". Similar to the way an eagle flies, so high above the mountains way up in the sky. The eagle never feels alone, but they always seem to enjoy the view from flying around at the top.

There is no need ever to envy anyone, be jealous of anyone, hate anyone, despise anyone, gossiping about anyone, busy bodying in anyone's personal business, disliking anyone, or even trying to be in the way of anyone's success. God is not slack concerning any promises, God is no respect of person, God is not the Arthur of confusion but peace, love, a sound mind and every man every woman will sow what they reap or folks often say reap what you sow. I encourage everyone to simply treat people with love and kindness. Whosoever God blesses, no man nor any woman could ever curse, don't forget that. In any event, we should provoke one another to love to do good works. Everyone will not speak well of you, if they did, watch out. If God, be for you who is it or what is it can be against you. Stay motivated! Too easy, like fried chicken too greasy.

We all should be too busy working on our own selves to be concerned about the petty things. Because no matter what, when it is a person's time to shine there's nothing no one could do. No weapon that is formed against us shall prosper, this is so real and so true. Bottom line, we are worth every blessing from the Mercy of God and much more if we would just allow these beliefs to rain over our hearts and overtake our minds the richness of God's glory. We'll worry less and pray more.

It's more blessing to give than to receive: I was leaving church and shortly made a stop to grab something for dinner. I happened to see a homeless guy walking on the streets of Berkeley with a cart. I pulled over to ask if he as hungry, he applied that he was. I stopped my truck to share my dinner with the homeless guy, gave him some water and some money. I asked him his name, he told me Stanley. I said how long have you been in this condition? He said for fifteen years, I ask what happened? He said he lost his mom and that led to him given up on himself and his life. I told him that I lost both my mom and my sister so I understand. I also shared with him that he will make it after regaining his confidence, self esteem and courage. To believe in yourself again, he started to smile with a sign of hope. I could tell that he was really hungry because as I was pulling away I looked in my rear view mirror and he was chopping it up like a piece of steak. That touched me! Jesus declares, if we do these things unto the lest of these my brethren we are doing it unto him. What ever is done in the secret God will reward us openly. Keep giving because what measure you share or put out, it will be measured to you again or in return.

Together we stand, lest divided we will fall. It really doesn't matter what the color of our skin is. We are One team, One family and One fight in this marvelous sight of God.

What goes for one, goes for us all. We must forgive all those who have hurt us in any kind of way, anyone who has betrayed you, used you, spoke false words out on you, trespassed against you, threw your name in the dirt and the mud. Whatever it is, forgive ; and feel those heavy burdens loosen you and fly away.

As A Retired Soldier

Its hard to believe the 26 years 4 months has come and gone for me. I'll never forget, we are trained to defend and to be the first one on the hill, taking down the enemy before the enemy takes us down. Fit to fight, trained to lead, to stay alert and be alive, not to leave anyone behind, we go to war together, we all come back home safely together, we won't be defeated, we will win! Thank you Army!

Theory's of life: God allow the male lion to be the king of the beast and the female lion to be the queen of the beast, for a purpose. They both are not the biggest, the tallest or the strongest. Instead, they both have a very strong heart, their heart is stronger than any animal because they will not run away. Their fearless and not fearful! To all the ones who enjoy bullying people through their size, through money, through words, or anything; remember only the strong survive and will rise after getting picked on. Negative words should never have an impact over the positive things in your life.

Life is a process: when you are in your twenties, you are entering into a world of uncertainty you are learning who you are, what you want to be and where you want to go in your life. In the thirties after shaking off the disappointments, healing from the scares and bad wounds it's defining you and preparing you to be a better person while building characteristic skills keeping your tools sharpened. In the forties you should be where you want to be and need to be in your life all the what if's and should I's must be over. In the fifties, sixties and beyond you should be completed, settled and ready to have life so smooth and enjoying the sun rise, the sunshine, and the sun setting for the day.

To the military friends and families: it's been nearly 9 years, I still have my battles with PTSD, those terrible nightmares, the sleepless nights and many months from restless nights of firing at the enemy, knocking him down, he gets up charging at me with a knife. The enemy gets close enough to stab me in the side of my six pack. I got up out of my bed to see where the blood is in my bed. I take a walk through the living room to try and shake that horrible nightmare off. About 30 minutes later, I fall back to sleep just to end up right back at the same horrible nightmare where it left off at. There are so many times, when those terrible nightmares attack me, I have to gather myself, my mind and try to remember, am I safe at home in the states or am I locked and loaded, and ready to protect our soldiers, marines, airmen, navy and civilians from the enemies fire. We were all serving together at the prison.

This was around 3:30 am in the morning. How bizarre is this, to still have this mental injury haunting me around and hitting me without any written notice or announcement to say, I'm here. So in order to help myself fight and treat this mental injury, I am man enough, a retired soldier enough, to speak with a counselor. And get the needed assistance provided for my stable mental condition. This doesn't mean anyone is crazy, but from being in a traumatic hostile environment for that long length of time as we endured while in Iraq will and does affect all of our service men and women.

If, you are experiencing the same type of issues or perhaps in a different way; take my advise, get help. We deserve it and it's part of our benefits. We are left with some psychological scares and wounds that need to be addressed and healed. Our country owe us, because we paid for it, by going to war.......

12

Relationships

I am so baffled to see how many men and women are so broken from the inside of their hearts by their past relationships. Some, if not many have allowed people to destroy their self esteem, their drive and the will to be better. The confidence, the courage, the love, and many times the faith. Someone will and can get lost in the midst of this horrible nightmare, it's like a bottomless pit you may have such a hard time getting out of. The key element into making things better, is to learn how to heal. Take some time away from dating and try to rediscover who you are. So imperative. You have to learn how to move in the direction of positivity, by way of making some healthy moves such as speaking with a therapist for support, try exercising, go for a nature walk to get all that frustration and bitterness out. Read the bible, read self healing productive books, find yourself again, believe in you again, lastly fast and pray.

Too often, I have noticed people fall into the trap of trying to get with someone else to ease their pain, when in fact it's a rebound and dating the next person so soon will not heal you, or separate you from the heartaches of suffering, but it will prolong your healing process within your heart and your mind. I find, we have so many confused and lost type of people today, destroyed from many heartbreaks and disappointments even years of devastations while depleting every layer of hope until you must get a grip and take charge of your inner man or inner woman.

Do not allow anyone or anything to take away your Joy. It really takes God, to amend a broken heart and heal one back together again. To all the men, every woman you see is not for you, when you are finished fishing for every fish in the sea, playing around with different women's hearts, tired of bumping your head in the same spot just to realize that hurts from doing the same thing over and over, healed from the dramatic heartaches and bad experiences, ready to be one on one with just one lady, your life is completely in order consisting of a home or a nice spacious apartment, the car, the career, the finances looking all good like you're going to Hollywood, benefits to cover a whole family, with all the necessary components in place, then you are ready.

Your heart will tell you so because we as men must provide the cement details and create a way to be the leader of the family. However, there is one woman waiting on you when you are, least expected. To all the women all the ladies, every man you run across, is not for you. Only, when you are completely healed from the heartbreaks, your past is over said and done, you have this very strong feeling of expecting a brighter present, future and forever more, your good and your bad experiences has allowed you to grow for the next level in your life, you can see a man out somewhere and it brings a smile from within, if your heart will be more receptive to trust and love again, you are ready.

When that man you do meet, can see the intellectual capacity and the understanding of your mind and see the direction of your lovable heart and not the outside of your appearance (your classy sexy body) only, he could be the One man you have been asking God for. Such an amazing position to be in with your mate, to experience the closeness and the unconditional love like the sun shining over your shoulder keeping you warm all day long. Like brown gravy and rice next to some smothered chicken or smothered steak on a plate cooking on a Sunday Soul food day with the family. The hope still remains.

As far as dating is concerned, I highly recommend that we should be more prepared to offer someone something just in case the connection is mutual and the feelings are beginning to grow strong towards each other. When we were in combat, no one was able to hit the ground running without being prepared with their weapons, ammo, protective mask, chemical suits, Kevlar, first aid kits, extra uniforms, boots, protective vest with plates, duffle bags, rucksack, sleeping bags, sleeping mat, toiletries, socks, under shirts, underwear, a couple of MREs, and money in their pockets. This may appear to be a bit much, but dating someone takes all of this and then some, because your mate deserves the best and nothing lest.

No more of this 20/80, 40/60 or even 50/50 madness. The proper fair goal of the true love percentage is 100/100, simply because those other fraction laws are not working for anyone, everybody is repeatedly falling way too short leaving an unbalanced couple crying the blues over the unfairness of the love rules.

If, a man or a woman cannot give you all of them, then they do not deserve your love and are not worth wasting your valuable time. When you find out in the beginning what a person is working with and you don't like it, why stay? Do yourself a favor and move on, no gain no loss.

With men, we are a very hard creature to understand. We take so long to express ourselves, we take forever to commit and stay loyal. I really believe, it's because of fear and for not being mentally prepared to go face to face with only one woman. The solution to this issue is experience, getting focused and being disciplined. We have to learn how to be more content and realize when a phenomenal woman comes your way, this doesn't happen everyday of your life.

Men, treat that fabulous Queen, like the way she deserves to be treated the same way you would love and take care of yourself. Keep in mind, temptation comes around all the time. The thought of your Queen, the true love that you share and the discipline will fight and keep those temptations under control; along with help from the Lord will help you to be strong enough to resist and to overcome.

When, your Queen mean something dear to you, we as men fight for them. Men, build up enough trust to minimize your insecurities and keep those crazy jealousy traits buried. Jealousy and insecurities will chase anyone completely away because we don't own each other, everyone is loaned by God in the first place. When we don't respect, trust and love the one God has sent you, you will loose that person.

God doesn't set up anyone for failure or even waste his goods on anyone. He's still in control and when we don't take care of what he gives us; just like he has the power and authority to give it, he has that the same power and authority to take it all away.

So, in other words; what you won't do, someone else will do. Only because everyone is patiently waiting on that special person to enter into their life and God understands to supply our needs.

Dating is a compromising and improvising healthy experience, as men we are made to provide and to protect. Going on a first date, men are always expected to lead the way and make the first step by treating and showing the lady, you can take care of her and keep everyone safe while you are out together.

Now, this may seem a little unbalanced but, the woman will get the main part of the stick and the man may get the short end of the stick, sort of like she gets the majority of the closet and the man gets the smallest portion of the closet. It is ok, this doesn't mean while dating someone exclusively she is to become complacent and forget to reciprocate by not showing the man she's out with, that he is cared for and appreciated, men have feelings too.

In the beginning stages of dating, if a man begins to feel taken advantage of, and each time he's out with the same lady, he notices when the bill comes to the table, she's looking around at the ceiling like a bird is of the restaurant. That man will come through your front door and leave out the back door without you knowing anything, his intention is to not look back and never to return. Next time you look up, he's not around because he's gone. You've chased that good man away, men have difficult times trusting and being open by nature anyhow, so ladies, treat the man and show the man you are dating how you want to be treated as well.

Keep in mind, there is someone ready to meet you where you are, in the area and aspects of your successful life......Its a beautiful thing to experience and share with someone, when the both of you can agree on having the same things in common and have the same things achieved, but in a different positive way to discuss the details of each individual's personal story...It's magnificent.

"God, doesn't give us the half pie of a blessing. He gives us the whole pie of a blessing."

13

The Right Approach to Life It's Yours to Enjoy

Of course, to be a successful individual among your peers, your colleagues, your family and your friends. There is so much work, sacrifice, effort and time to put in while at times this may cause you to burn up some midnight oil and have a few cups of some vanilla creamers mixed with coffee to get the job done.

It's a joy, full of excitement to watch someone make it, in life. This can consist of the job that pays a six digit salary, or finally graduating from college after pursuing that BA, Masters or P.hD; or perhaps, receiving that much needed promotion after getting passed over a few times. Also, getting that first acting job to start your life in making movies, while saving up for years to finally get that dream home or that dream car. Which ever one comes to pass, this is the time to welcome all the good things waiting in store, just for you. The motivation is not to take what's not yours, but the motivation is to simply get yours too. Keep in mind, when you don't get it the right way, you'll lose it the wrong way. No one wants that!

Just in case, you may have forgotten or don't quite understand. It takes praying, it takes being proactive, it takes being steadfast and being unmovable. Sometimes you might get tired and get frustrated at the same time. This is ok, everyone and everybody can agree on this, that it will take some work to get where you desire to go in your life.

This is important, you only appreciate the things that you had to earn and work hard for, than someone giving it to you for free out of the clear blue sky. Only because of the earned efforts and all the hard work it took for you to get it. You will value it a little bit more. When someone does give you something and you know within your heart, you didn't do anything to deserve it, you won't appreciate it, it has no sentimental value. Trust me on this.

Everyday, when we awake to see a new day; we should make it our duty and our job without any pressure or stress added to do our best, continue to be honest, to be right, to stay humble and to enjoy what the Lord has given to us to survive with. This earth is blessed with so many perfect gifts and perfect things from the Lord. All He want us to do is not forget him and forget where it came from. Every good gift and every perfect gift does come from above.

God smiles, in fact it pleases him to give you the desires from your heart. Approach life the right way, it's yours; to enjoy.......

14

Lessons Learned
Just a Cue, a Clue, and a Hint

It takes respect to get respect. When we don't stand for what's right and what's wrong, we fall down to anything, and that brings confusion.

As adults, we have to continue being accountable and responsible for our own actions. People are always watching, and our youth see us too.

We should stop saying, "I'm grown," as if no one can ever tell us anything else while on earth. To me it sounds arrogant and disrespectful. As long as you are alive, there is yet something else and more to learn. The respectful thing to say is "I am an adult," or "We are adults."

I remember telling my mom, "I'm eighteen." She looked at me and said she didn't care how old I became, she would always be my mother. "And you'll never be older than I am." My mom shut me down real quick. My theory: Mothers are always right, so listen to them and respect them.

Words are powerful. They can save a life, or they can destroy a life. Evil communications will corrupt good manners. Stay far away from negative people, surround yourself with healthy, positive people because this will promote growth. Plus, it's way less stressful.

No matter what's going on in this world today, God is and will always be in control. The earth is the Lord's, the fullness thereof and they that dwell therein. This means everything and everybody.

Be more thankful and grateful to the Lord for the things he has already done, for the things he is getting ready to do and for what he is working on right now.

Continue to ask the Lord to bless your going out and your coming back in. He is our refuge, our present help in the time of any type of trouble.

God will prepare you for your blessings, and to receive the good things that you are so rightfully deserving of. His blessings are rich, and they do not add any sorrow in your life.

Sometimes in life, things will be uncomfortable in order for one to be comfortable in their own personal life. What I mean, and what I am trying to convey is this: always pay your way, stop looking for the easy way out of things, enough with asking people to always hook you up. Plant your own seeds and water your own garden. You only get back whatever it is you put out in life.

This may seem a little strange or different, but in life, sometimes you will be in a place where someone doubts you, doesn't believe in you, doesn't encourage you, ain't never got anything good to say about you. So my advice: try much harder, work out that much harder, work hard at what you want for yourself that much harder, just to prove to those few unbelievers that you will succeed. These kinds of people do keep you on your heels or keep you on the edge. It's just to sharpen up your tools, sharpen up your mind, because tools can get dull. Then your mind can become complacent and cause you to lose all your good thoughts. These kinds of people, believe it or not, motivate me.

"Sometimes in life, when it looks like you're going to lose, don't fret or don't falter because God has a way of turning that thing around just in the nick of time for you and make you a winner." We walk in faith and not by sight.

Those of you pursuing careers throughout various occupations; making the best changes for your life; buying that first new home, which is an amazing investment; getting married and ready to start a new family, being on the journey road of traveling and seeing the world, or even starting your own business—I have to admit, this all sounds good, and this will have you nervous and shaking at the knees. But, utilize your drive and get it done. There have always been people before, during, and after who have felt the same kind of emotions but wanted their lives to be better and didn't want to let anything go until after their mission was completed.

Learn how to be impressed with yourself, without forgetting what it took for you to get there; no one can honestly celebrate you more than you can. You were the one who made the necessary sacrifices and changes and put in the work to bring it all together. Others see only your finished product.

To everyone, get those credit scores back up. It's literally hurting your future, your perfect chance to purchase that new home or start a business, and it's hurting those relationships, preventing them from being healthy, stronger, and happily everlasting. No one should ever have to pay the debt that you accumulated prior to getting married. Get disciplined, and get your credit file together. It's only fair, and you'll appreciate that in the long run.

Parents, let your kids be kids. Teach them the fundamentals of life, teach them about the morals and values of life, teach them how to cook, do chores, show them how to clean a room and keep it that way, teach and show them how to be responsible. Teach them about life's ups and downs. There's going to be some ups and a whole lot of downs regarding life. The sun is not going to shine every day because there are going to be some rainy days. Teach them the importance of the word *yes* and the true meaning of the word *no*. Help them to understand how to be a kid because they are not adults; it's too much for them to comprehend. Provide the best solutions to their problems in life and give the kids a chance to grow up mentally, because physically, they are growing—it's natural, and it is a part of life. Teach the kids how to comb their hair, teach them how to fix themselves and look neat wearing their clothes. Lastly, teach them their manners, how to be more respectful, and how to be obedient. We are losing far too many kids today. Raise them in a way that when they get older, they will always respect their parents. Parents, you have to teach them and show them how to be a kid first and prepare them to be an adult when the time is near.

"The Lord, can and will do anything in our lives, without failing you or letting you down." He is the only wise, King of Kings, and he is mighty! He told Peter to go to the edge of the sea, the first fish that you catch open up the fish's mouth, and you'll find some money to give to the tax collector, because it was tax season. Because our God is great! God can still heal all manners of diseases, sicknesses in the land, and perform miracles just to prove his love for us. He's able to heal cancer, hypertension, depression, diabetes, PTSD, broken hearts, confusion in the mind, loneliness, no money in the bank, when and if your telephone disconnects while you're waiting for your next paycheck. He is able to restore your joy, restore your faith and hope, restore your peace, and renew your mind by comforting you. He is able to create the right spirit within you and give you favor with man. No matter what it is, he can take care of it all.

"All the works and the deeds that we do for others, let's do it unto the Lord and watch him reward you over and over again." He will allow the sun to shine brightly for you, like it does during the noonday.

As we continue to live our lives and be an example to others, here are a few things more to learn: we will see some things that we have never seen before, we will hear some things that we have never heard before, we will think about some things that we have never thought of before, and we will receive some blessings that we have never gotten before. All because God is so unlimited and so powerful.

We all at times, need someone to hear us and listen to us, to help us get back on track. Delivering some good ole advice to turn our lives back around without putting us down, but instead to build us up. Tell us something to shake us up, to wake up and get it together.

"Traveling along your journey, there will be moments when something huge or small may hit you and meet you face to face; stay strong in the heart and fight that bear or that lion. This determines how much you want your goals achieved."

❧ 15 ❧

Paradise and Joy from a Sunday Love
A compelling story

A very handsome man in the military, by the name of Benjamin, in and out of a few relationships prior to a combat tour that changes his life forever. He's preparing for deployment and begin to date someone while eventually falling in love with the lady. After sending her money, sending her expensive gifts, paying on a few bills of hers and giving the support that she deserves. While, he was in war keeping the soldiers safe and fighting off the enemy in combat.

It's time to come back home from a very stressful, lengthy and dangerous tour. Just to learn, the woman he fell in love with decides to walk away from him.

Feeling down for a while, he gets enough strength from God to rise back up again and begin to heal from the emotional scares.

One day, leaving church on a Sunday afternoon he drives over to Jack London Square a popular area in downtown Oakland and discovers a farmers market event taking place. He gets out of his vehicle and walks around, shortly he spots a very classy, attractive stunning woman with her legs crossed on a bench reading a book.

First he looks at her to pick up some eye contact and try to access the move on how to approach the attractive woman. Immediately, a burst of confidence and courage overtakes his mind, heart and body. So, he walks up to the pretty lady and introduces himself and say how are you? My name is Benjamin and with a warm friendly smile from the attractive woman, she says my name is Rebecca. He feels completely at ease right away and sits on the other side of the bench.

Timing is everything, the conversation starts out with discussing the book she was reading, into discussing everyday life, leading into the current events to engaging in some deep and personal issues about each other's family.

As we all know, when you are having a fabulous time with someone, the time starts to slip away until the time doesn't even matter anymore. They both noticed the beautiful sight of the sun setting and the start of a clear view evening lighting up the blue sky was on the way.

Just the two of them, had so many, many things in common and the connection, the chemistry grew stronger and stronger until they didn't want the night to end without exchanging numbers and emails, but as quiet as kept, Benjamin didn't want the presence of her glow to end either.

Meanwhile, that following week Benjamin decides to give Rebecca a call to say hello and to ask her out to dine at this elegant restaurant in Concord, Ca for a very romantic evening full of fun and laughter, she excepted. Let's say, they went on more dates spent more time together and countless hours, moments over the phone which created something extraordinary for the both of them. They were getting close and closer as the days and weeks turned into months. He finally gets invited to meet her family and what a fabulous and sensational treat. Her family was so good to him, felt he knew them for a long time. He returns the same gesture and invites her to be around his family and let's say, his family was shouting for joy over her.

The Two would attend church together, sporting events together, travel on weekend getaways, hike and bike together, cook some nice romantic evening meals together. By this time 6 months later, the two are speaking about love, commitment, exclusiveness, finances, credit scores, loyalty, support, making their own family.

He knew, she was the one when he would be out shopping at a mall and come out with bags full of surprises for her. He knew, she was the one when the two of them would be at a family event filled with people and when he would see her across the room the only person and the only voice he heard was hers. In spite of everyone else laughing talking and having a great time. With a smile he blows her a kiss, she blows him a kiss in return, he takes it and places it on his lips then on his chest, she starts to blush.

A full year of dating, things have gotten quite serious between the two. One day the two decides to take a ride out together to have dinner at a secluded romantic restaurant near the water. He parks and walks around to her side of the car to open the door for her to get out and they begin walking and holding hands near the restaurant, he stops to reach in his pocket and pulls out a 24 karat diamond ring. He kneels down on both knees to ask the beautiful classy attracted lady to do him the honors and marry him? With tears of unspeakable joy coming down her face and giving him that gleam and sparkle from her eyes, she says yes.

Sitting at the table across from Rebecca, Benjamin goes to say, he wants to give her every bit of him and Rebecca tells him, she wants to give him all of her. Benjamin tells Rebecca, I love you and I am in love with you, Rebecca says baby I have felt this affection for you from the first time we met but I didn't want to chase you away. Benjamin says I will support your hopes and dreams, you are my fire and all of my desire. My Queen and Valentine everyday in every way, I will prepare for you breakfast in bed, have the bubble bath ready with the candles lit. We can plan some weekend getaways, spend family time together, I will bring you surprises to make your day. Bring you home some Victoria Secrets to feel sexy and classy. While keeping you safe, protected, providing for you and be there always at your rescue and defeat. Rebecca ask him, are you trying to sweep me off of my feet?

He replies, not only that but I'm trying carry you to the stars and the moon too, for the rest of my life.

Rebecca blushes and left feeling speechless.

After a night of excitement, Rebecca spreads the news to her family and her family starts to celebrate with her leading up to the wedding.

In between the wedding rehearsals, picking out the perfect cake, sending out the invitations. The lovely couple were able to squeeze in some time to do some house hunting together.

Looking over 3 homes in a week they have decided to purchase this immaculate 6 bedroom, 5 bathroom, 4 car garage, 2 leveled, with an opened view, tall ceiling, fully loaded gated home together. He signed his name on the title and she did the same.

6 months preparing for The Wedding and with the wedding planner, this was Benjamin's first wedding and this was Rebecca's first wedding. So, she wanted the wedding of her dreams and he gave it to her. The color scheme was chosen together and the couple went all out to satisfy each other's style and taste.

Rebecca meets her mom, her sisters, and the bridesmaids one evening at the Vera Wang collection bridal store to try out some fabulous weeding gowns. Each gown Rebecca tried on were the perfect fit, so her choice was for that romantic appeal with her man Benjamin in mind, settled her decision with ease. Rebecca's mom Mrs Wilson tells her, she is so excited to have Benjamin as a son in law and welcomes him with open arms to the family. Rebecca begins to drop a few tears and tells her mom, how much she loves her some Benjamin.

When while, Benjamin, Rebecca's father, the best man and the grooms were all getting fitted for their suits and tuxedos. The guys were having so much fun hanging out and enjoying the evening together. From all the excitement in the air, Benjamin pulls Rebecca's father Mr Wilson to the side and thanks him for giving away his daughter to him and making him feel like a son in law. Mr Wilson tells Benjamin, the pleasure is all mine, and he could not have ever asked for a better person for Rebecca.

Benjamin and Rebecca spent a very nice pre-wedding close family and friends evening dinner together, to enjoy everyone's positive energy and love before that day of the glorious wedding. Everyone loved the dinner, the nice gifts and the closeness of the intimate settings. It was 9:30 pm, they made a toast and ended the dinner to be prepared for the wedding that next day.

It's 10:00 am, the morning of the wedding day. The wedding is scheduled to begin at 4:00 pm

Rebecca wanted to captivate the guest with a stunning evening dress to be remembered for a life time and she did. She wore this hand sewn detailed off white tone gown that fit perfect all over that beautiful body. He wore this fitted tan 4 button suit that complimented her gown with sure elegance.

As Benjamin awaits Rebecca's presence at the front of the church near the altar standing tall and looking good, the music plays, the guest stand to their feet and there she is, the apple of his eye walking down the middle to receive her King. She was walking with her father, but she was the only one he was looking at. While looking at her, he begins to feel weak at the knees but he maintains his composer. His best man ask, are you ok, he replies I'm ok, just ready to receive and hold my Queen. You could hear all the ooo's and the aaaaaaaw's as she approaches the altar. He reaches for her hands and here we go, the Bishop says, let us pray.

Their vows during the ceremony were intimate and very romantic. Benjamin shares wth Rebecca, you are my first, my only and my last woman forever. My cup runneth over for you. You are compassionate, amiable, very empathetic, exuberant, so affectionate and sexy to me. I will hold you, kiss you, adore you, cherish, protect and provide for you. I will support your endeavors, your hopes and your dreams. I am so in love with you pretty lady, you give me joy.

Rebecca shares with Benjamin, you are my first, my only and my last man forever baby. I want you to be my lover, my best friend, my confidant, my traveling partner. I will support your ambitions, your hopes and your dreams. You so strong and good to me baby, you always make me feel like a brand new woman, you are passionate, considerate, sensible to my needs. I am so in love with you handsome man, you give me butterflies.

The ceremony was lavished and very extravagant beyond anyone's imagination with so much soothing great music, a live band, the food was off the chain, the wedding planner did a splendid job on everything, the guest and celebrities were surprised with hidden expensive and costly gifts for sharing a part of this glorious event and witnessing, true love never fails. The night was filled with so much love in the air until no one wanted the night to end.

The newly wedded couple were prepared to take their honeymoon flight to Paris at 6:00 am, the next morning and how can one say, this was a trip of a lifetime. 7 night stay, expenses paid and a honeymoon to remember.

Who would have ever thought, the handsome man could ever find the perfect love again. He wondered if he would ever trust again. Although, the thoughts of caring and sharing were always in his head and in the middle of his heart, the top and the bottom too. True love is Powerful, trust is inevitable. All of this Joy because of a Sunday love.

The two made the most beautiful God sent family and are happier than anything and anyone in life. He wrote her a song, called it " You are Great".

After returning back home from one of the most romantic places on earth in Paris, the lovely newlyweds are anxiously ready to settle down into their amazing new home.

You can tell the sparks and the fireworks were still lighting up the sky and the true love they were feeling for each other grew stronger and stronger because while he was showering to get comfortable, fresh and clean , she walked into their spacious shower to join him and wanted to share another romantic moment while the water was steaming hot and hitting their bodies together.

The lovely couple, just could not get enough of one another. They both indulged the rest of the night with passion, romance, closeness, and bonded like never before.

It's morning time, Benjamin gets up takes a shower, puts on his robe and walks downstairs to the kitchen to prepare her first breakfast in bed.

On the menu; he prepares turkey bacon, seasoned fresh hash brown potatoes, lightly buttered grits, lightly scrambled eggs, lightly brown wheat toast with strawberry jelly, fresh fruits and a tall glass of orange juice.

Everything was smelling so good, until he could hear her asking baby, do you need any help? With a smile he replies sweetheart I'm finished and I'm coming upstairs to bring you some breakfast in bed.

He walks up to the California King size bed and as he lay her breakfast tray on her lap, they both kiss to start the morning out right.

She then, begin to cry and explains no one has ever done this for me before. He says pretty lady, the way I start out with you, is the only way I'm going take care of you, all I want and all I have is you.

From that day forward, everyday the lovely couple were doing exceptionally well.

About a month later, the couple had an appointment on a Thursday afternoon at the doctor's office and received some spectacular news. They are expecting; this was his first and this was her first, so you know this is going to be something really special.

She could hardly wait to share the great news with her family and friends. Her parents, especially her mom and some other family members were at the house nearly everyday to be there and to show that they care. He didn't mind, because they were all excited about a new life coming to the family.

8 months later, the baby was on the way. Because the couple wanted to wait and find out if it's a boy or a girl towards the end for the delivery and praying for a healthy baby, the nervousness got stronger until the moment of the arrival of the baby. The doctors and the nursing staff were all ready to rock and roll. It was 6:00 pm, the baby was ready to come out. The delivery room packed with medical people all around, about 30 minutes later, the doctor announces, it's a boy!

Her parents, sisters, close friends were all present at the hospital to welcome their new baby son. It was so much joy and excitement in that hospital room. The baby boy was so handsome, head full of hair, eyes like his mom, little big hands like his dad. Her parents were standing by, it looked like her dad Mr Wilson wanted to break down and cry, but he didn't, he held it together.

Bringing a life into the world, is very remarkable how God allows life to be formed and created the way it is. God, is really awesome.....Benjamin and Rebecca named their son Joshua..

Finally, after a few days of recovering at the hospital from the new addition to the family, it's time for mommy and the new born son to come home. The proud and happy dad made sure that both families were at the new home to celebrate this special occasion, just for a short visit. The new mom had to get her rest and their new son Joshua was looking like, he did not want to be bothered. They make it home safely and everyone were cheering for the new addition to the family.

Rebecca's parents, sisters and few close friends were so genuine and caring to help the new mom in any way that they could. 6 months passes, the new baby son is growing, starting to recognize his grandparents and aunts. It's his 1st birthday, he received so many gifts, it felt Christmas. He's walking, into everything, crazy about his grandparents and aunts. They all just love him so much, the lovely newlywed couple are very proud parents and are extremely happy to be so in love with each other. Time surely flies, when you are enjoying life, the person you are with and having a great time.

Benjamin gathers everyone together in the family room part of the house, picks up his new son and tells everyone thank you. He expresses, you have made this part of our lives so incredible, with tears in his eyes he looks to his wife and say, you are amazing. I adore you, cherish you and I am so in love with you.

Benjamin also shares with her parents in front of everyone, your lovely daughter is my gift from God and I will continue to provide for her, protect her and love her unconditionally like never before.

The lovely Rebecca stands up and walks over to her proud husband and holds him with their son Joshua in his arms while they begin to share tears of happiness and joy together. After while, everyone was dropping a few tears and feeling the tenderness in the family room.

It is true, love does change a person, heals a person and grabs a person by the hand ; just to lead them to the one they are suppose to be with.....He waited all of his life for her and she waited all of her life, just for him; what a remarkable couple.

Paradise and Joy from a Sunday love....

~⟨ 16 ⟩~

Paradise and Joy from a Sunday love....

Life has been so amazing, so incredible for Benjamin, Rebecca and little Joshua. Over a year later, reminiscing about meeting the best woman God could have given from Heaven up above, where he allowed his angels to deliver such an astonishing woman who is perfect for him. Gave them the most gorgeous mind-blowing, jaw-dropping wedding that was literally wondrous.

Both Benjamin and Rebecca was so blessed to give birth to a very healthy, handsome baby boy. Everything has fallen in the right place at the right time for the two love birds until it was all worth the wait. Marriage is still honorable and ordained by God.

Benjamin has made plans to surprise Rebecca with a vacation trip to explore Europe and to celebrate their one year anniversary. So, he makes all the arrangements, purchased the airline tickets, made the hotel reservations and awaits for Rebecca to return home with Joshua from visiting her parents.

6:00 pm, that Thursday evening Rebecca calls and tells Benjamin, that her and Joshua are on their way home from her parents in about 15 minutes. Benjamin rushes up the stairs to light some candles, start the bubble bath with the water just right, the way Rebecca likes it. Then, he set the 2 dozen long stem red roses in a vase on her side of the bed to express his deep love for Rebecca to really make her night. Fellas, red roses are for love, yellow and pink roses are for friendship.

6:25 pm, Benjamin hears one of the garage doors opening, Rebecca makes it home safely and pulls right on in. Benjamin opens the door from the kitchen to the garages and with a smile he blows Rebecca a kiss, Rebecca blushes.

Benjamin helps out with unfastening Joshua from his car seat and rushes Rebecca inside and up the stairs because the candles are burning and the bubble bath is waiting on her.

Rebecca walks in the master room and see the 2 Dozen long stem red roses and breaks down with tears of happiness. Joshua walks over to her and say, mommy are you ok? Me and daddy love you! Benjamin says, honey let's walk in the master bathroom, again Rebecca is left speechless, after seeing the candles lit and bubble bath waiting on her. Benjamin says, I just want to show you that I love you, and to share and say I really care about you. Rebecca gets undressed and walks into the deep tub to enjoy her bubble bath and candles.

Benjamin and Joshua walks back into the master room, to retrieve the envelope with the flight arrangements and hotel reservations for their anniversary vacation trip to Europe. Benjamin hands the gift to Joshua to give to his mother. Rebecca opens the envelope reads the details and screams, Benjamin walks up to the tub, kisses Rebecca and say, pretty lady, this is all for you. Rebecca tells Benjamin baby, I am so in love with you, thank you baby.

8:30 pm, Benjamin takes Joshua to his bedroom, to give him a bath and to put him to sleep for the night.

Benjamin returns back to the master room shortly, after Joshua falls sound asleep. Rebecca looking extremely nice with her light blue satin and lace slip on with the matching robe just slightly above her knees looking so lovely and attractive like a movie scene from HBO. Benjamin leans in on Rebecca to give her a kiss and to feel the softness of her lips.

Benjamin and Rebecca's night of passion heats up more and more each time, and has gotten better and more better than ever. These two, just can't get enough of each other. Another special night to remember.

It's Saturday morning, the luggage bags are packed and loaded. Benjamin and Rebecca had made previous plans for Joshua to stay with her parents Mr. And Mrs. Wilson. Joshua ran into the arms of his grandfather and waved back as Benjamin and Rebecca as they getting into the car to leave for their trip.

Arriving at the airport, Benjamin and Rebecca are holding hands while waiting to get through the security check point. The security check team got the lovely couple through quickly, after taking a seat and waiting for the flight, Benjamin and Rebecca are so excited to be traveling together again.

Two hours later, it's time to board the plane. It's going to be a 16 hour flight to Frankfurt, Germany.

The flight to Frankfurt, Germany was smooth, long and exciting. Rebecca noticed that the flight was full of couples and started to enter act with the couple sitting behind her and Benjamin. Rebecca and the friendly lady were talking for about a good three hours.

Rebecca gets tired, turns back around in her seat, places her head on Benjamin's shoulder with a pillow and a blanket, then falls asleep. Benjamin was already asleep.

The pilot speaks into the intercom to everyone and says welcome to Frankfurt, Germany our landing time is approximately in one hour. Everyone starts to cheer and celebrate. The fasten your seat belt sign comes on and they are ready to come in for a landing. The pilot says, everyone please take your seat.

We have landed safely in Frankfurt, Germany. Benjamin and Rebecca retrieves their luggage, takes a ride in this very nice BMW taxi to the GrandHotel Hessischer Hof. This German hotel was striking, eye-catching and breathtaking. The hotel staff was so friendly, professional, the room occupied by Benjamin and Rebecca had a phenomenal view of the downtown buildings and a clear view lake to welcome their stay in Frankfurt, Germany.

The room was decorated with a classy, elegant style that made the couple feel right at home. Benjamin had so many plans to share with Rebecca, to give her the best time of her life. The plans were to dine at the most gorgeous restaurants in Europe, take a tour to sight see the castles, visit some architectural buildings and historical sites. Take a walk over to the art museums and Benjamin made arrangements to take a yacht to brace the clean fresh air of Europe and to enjoy the view of the Heidelberg castle. Benjamin took so many pictures for the memories to last for a life time.

Seven days has passed, Benjamin and Rebecca had so much fun, the time dissipated so fast until it was that time again to head over to the airport, board the plane and to return back home to the states.

The flight was full and filled with so many couples again. This is a coincidence Benjamin and Rebecca's seats are in front the same couple from the first flight into Europe, once again the ladies are chopping it up over their amazing trip and discussing all the activities and details that everyone enjoyed from the trip.

Two hours later, Benjamin was so exhausted he falls asleep, shortly afterwards Rebecca grabs a blanket and a pillow, then lays on Benjamin's shoulder and she is out like a light. Benjamin hears a little snoring coming from Rebecca, but that's alright, she was worn out completely from a specular trip in Europe.

16 hours later, the plane has landed safely back at the San Francisco International Airport. Everyone on board is cheering and celebrating for a nice flight back home to the states.

One hour later, Benjamin and Rebecca grabbed their luggage loaded up the Suv and headed home, it's 10:00 pm. The couple made it to the house safely, Rebecca calls her mother to check on Joshua and says she'll be there in the morning to pick him up.

Benjamin walks into the shower to relax and to feel better from that long trip from Europe. As he's getting out of the shower, Rebecca comes and ask him to stay in a little longer for her. Benjamin smiles and say ok baby. The shower ended up taking a while because the love moment started to take over with so much excitement and intimacy.

Rebecca whispers in Benjamin's ear that, I love you so much, Benjamin kisses Rebecca on the back of her neck and says, my love for you is forever and ever. Benjamin turns off the shower, dries Rebecca all over with a bath towel and then carries her to the Cal King bed. Rebecca softly tells Benjamin, you are so good to me honeybun, with a grin Benjamin says, always and forever sweet potato pie.

It's 2:00 am, in the morning. The couple turns on a movie, cuddles close together and falls asleep.

9:00 am, Rebecca and Benjamin both are getting dress and ready to pick up Joshua from her parents home. The couple pulls up in the driveway of Rebecca's parents home, they ring the door bell and can hear Joshua running to the front door.

Mrs Wilson opens the front door and Joshua is very excited to see his mom and dad. Everyone walks down to the family room and takes a seat to discuss the trip and engage in some family talk.

Mr and Mrs Wilson wanted to have brunch at a nearby cafe downtown, that serves their favorite meals, so the whole gang join in for an afternoon full of family time and enjoyment.

Benjamin has gotten quite closer than close with Rebecca's parents. Mr and Mrs Wilson has filled all the loop holes and emptiness that Benjamin has experienced for the last 20 years. It has been a very long time coming, but well worth the wait. And also, Benjamin is like a son that Mr Wilson has never had. That's special.

That's how God does it, when he blesses us, he makes up for all the lost time, as if it was never lost at all....God, controls the time too!

After 2 1/2 hours of playing catch up with her parents and other family members, Rebecca leans over to Benjamin and ask, are you ready to go? Benjamin gets Joshua together, the entire table stands up, say their good-byes and gives their hugs and starts to walk toward the parking lot to drive home.

As Benjamin and Rebecca are driving home, she reaches her hand across to hold his hand, turns around and see that Joshua has fallen asleep in his car seat. The couple makes it home safely, puts Joshua to bed and turns on a movie and relaxes on the sofa in the family room together, until Rebecca begins to drift off to sleep.

Benjamin is the only one awake, so he turns to ESPN, to catch up on all the sports.....

Still Paradise and Joy from a Sunday love.....over a year later!

Benjamin and Rebecca are doing exceptionally well together with their earnings and good living lifestyle. He's retired from the military and was able to invest in a few stocks that worked out perfect for him prior to transitioning into the civilian life. Rebecca on the other hand is a well defined professional and experienced Pediatrician Doctor with over 18 years under her practice.

Rebecca has finally returned back to work after a long extensive time away from having her son Joshua. Her team and the support of her colleagues has made the wedding, the new born of her son all worth the while.

Everyone was so happy, elated and overjoyed to see Rebecca back on the hospital floors once again. She heard, felt the cheers and love from nearly the entire hospital. Many were teary eyed, and welcomed Rebecca with open arms.

Rebecca has received numerous and high prestigious awards for her work as a Pediatrician Doctor, when visitors come to visit Rebecca at her office, there are times people are amazed of the achievements earned by Rebecca. The display of all her awards are neatly placed all around her office on the walls and on her desk. Benjamin is in the office today and shares with Rebecca, that she is his hero.

Rebecca receives a call, a baby just came into the hospital with trouble breathing and need immediate care. Rebecca has to leave to take care of the emergency. Now, that's a doctor who cares and loves her work. Benjamin understands, they kiss and he heads out to let the doctor perform her job.

It's 7:00 pm on a Monday evening, Rebecca is home from work, Benjamin has cooked one of Rebecca's favorite meals; turkey meatloaf with gravy, fresh mashed potatoes with onions, seasoned broccoli with shrimp on top and some lightly buttered cornbread.

Benjamin, Rebecca and Joshua are enjoying a nice evening meal together at the dinner table, Joshua has been asking about getting a little puppy. Benjamin and Rebecca start to look at each other and chuckle.

Later that evening, Benjamin has the bubble bath ready just right for Rebecca. While Rebecca is soothing and relaxing in the tub, Benjamin starts to look up and find on the Internet what kind of family puppy they should bring into their home, so he discusses with Rebecca what kind of puppy do she want to be around Joshua.

The very next day, Benjamin with Rebecca's permission and consent have decided to purchase a baby adorable tan looking female Shih Tzu. Benjamin, Rebecca and Joshua drives over to the SPCA that evening to pick up the new addition to the family.

Benjamin parks the car and walks around to open the door for Rebecca and to get Joshua out of his car seat and then walks in to see their new family member. Immediately Joshua runs over to the cage and spots out the little puppy and the little puppy takes to him right away. The owner opens the cage to grab the little Shih Tzu and Joshua hugs the little puppy tightly and he would not let go.

Benjamin and Rebecca names the little baby Shih Tzu, Sunset. The family finally had everything taken care of, got Sunset washed, groomed and the shots completed. Loaded up back into the car and drives home with their new baby pet.

Joshua could hardly wait to play with his new family member, the minute they were able to get home, Joshua and Sunset are already playing with each other like it has been years of knowing each other. Benjamin and Rebecca picked the best pet to be a part of Joshua's life.

It has gotten late, Rebecca goes to check on Joshua and Sunset in the family room, and finds the both of them curled up together on the couch fast asleep. Rebecca calls Benjamin to the family room to see the two fast asleep and Benjamin takes a picture of Joshua and Sunset looking worn out sleeping good.

Family means everything, the values and the tradition, the closeness and the togetherness, the love and the support, the joy and the excitement of sharing your life with someone special is so incredible. Adding the perfect pet sure does make life amazing. Children gives us the right perspective of a loving home. There's a valuable lesson to learn from having a happy home, everything just fits perfect and in place.

Two people can agree and walk together, forever.

Paradise and much Joy from a Sunday Love.....The end

I remember when, life was so much fun
Saturday morning and Saturday afternoon
Come back home:

I remember when, every Saturday morning life was so much fun. All the funny cartoons, would come on. We would laugh so hard at the Flintstones, Casper the friendly ghost, the Jetsons, Woody wood pecker, Ma and Pa bear family, Leghorn foghorn, the Arabian Knights, the Thundercats, Droopy, Scooby Do, all the Super Friends, all the Looney Tunes, Spider-Man and the amazing friends, He-man, Richie Rich, Mighty Mouse, Johnny Quest, The Pink Panther, The Plastic Man, Popeye the Sailor Man, Huckleberry Hound, Yogi Bear, Top Cat, Wally Gator, Tom and Jerry, The Secret Squirrel, Atom Ant, The Hillbilly Bears, Winsome Witch, Squiddly Diddly, The Banana Splits, The Wacky Races, The Harlem Globetrotters, Speed Buggy, Jabberjaw, Dynomutt Dog Wonder, Captain Caveman, The Smurfs, Godzilla, The Great Grape Ape, Goober and the Ghost Chasers, Hong Kong Phooey, The Herculoids, The Perils of Penelope Pitstop, Precious Pupp, and Shazzan.

I may have missed a few, but this was our Saturday morning...

I remember when, every Saturday afternoon and during the week nights was so much fun. All the funny movies,would come on. We would get educated, laugh and learn something about life. By watching; Jerry Lewis, Dean Martin and Sammy Davis Jr, the Three Stooges, the Little Rascals, Abbot and Costello, Good times, Happy Days, The Jeffersons, Creature feature, The Love Boat, Fantasy Island, Sanford and Son, Different Strokes, A Different World, What's Happening, Family Matters, The Brady Bunch, That's My Mama, Benson, Hart to Hart, Lavern and Shirley, Mork and Mindy, Bob Hope, I Love Lucy, The Monsters, The Beverly Hillbillies, Laurel and Hardy.

Now, all of these cartoons, comedy movies and shows were the must see TV, in those days. Everyone were fully engaged, attentive to the laughter and growth that we received.

18

True Love never fails; It's Flawless

Out of all the love in this world, God's love is the most powerful and strongest emotion known to mankind. Love is much stronger than hate. Love heals, love reveals how passionate God is to his people, love is very positive, love diminishes anything that's negative. Love builds up, love can restore and renew the building that was torn down.

The earth is moaning and groaning, God feels your pain and hears your cry...He's still, in control of the universe and the world. We do have a high priest, who can be touched with the feelings of our infirmities or afflictions.

Love is about doing and being what's right, love works no ill to your neighbor, love treats everyone the same, true love will never change, love forgives, love can be unconditional, the true love of God is original, love works in strange places, true love is for all ages, love is openness, true love takes away the foolishness.

Love is kind, true love is not blind, love is for real, true love is sincere and it doesn't have any fear, love can sometimes hurt, true love still works, love is flawless, God's love is endless, love is mercy and grace, true love will cover all mistakes.

Love is friendly, true love keeps the family, love is always and forever, true love will keep your marriage together, love is so strong, true love will help you to hold on, love is caring and sharing, true love opens your understanding, God is still full of love, sent from the heaven's up above..

Love brings affection, true love shows compassion, love is patient, love is happiness, true love is showing friendliness, love is limitless, true love won't leave us comfortless, love is romantic, true love is connected, love causes one to grow, true love sits high but looks low, love is not rushing, true love is trusting, love won't turn you away, true love is here to stay.

Love is for every sister, every brother-God's love is meant for every color, it doesn't matter who you are and where you're from.......love is not selfish, true love is honest and selfless. Love is understanding, true love is always giving.

"True Love never fails; it's Flawless". Love is so beautiful to have, true love is amazing to see for all. Love is a special touch, that means so much....what kind of love do you have?

God's love, is the true perfect love that has all the answers for the concerns and the issues for the problems we are facing in our nation today....no one loves us more than the Lord because he gave his life on Calvary for us all! Now, that is love...

Only the true love that we share towards each other, will work and will last...this is how the victory is won and this is how the spirit of hate is defeated... together with love, we must stand and lay all of our differences to the side.

True love never fails; it's Flawless!

My Thesis

The Conclusion

In conclusion, always speak well about yourself, you are what you say you are, so make it all good. Take command and better care of your body, it's a reflection of who you are. Speak kind words, speak healthy words, speak positive words and speak life back into your life. Generate a form of motivation, inspiration, dedication, discipline and determination to be what your heart desires. No one has the authority to prevent you from moving forward, only you and God can control that......It's in you, to persevere, to achieve your ambitions and to fulfill your purpose.

As we potentially discover more about ourselves along this successful journey, it's ok to do a recon, assess all the situations and conduct an after action review to create a better way of learning from any failures or mistakes. Just to do better next time, just to build the confidence and the hope, and to be a better person. Keep in mind, there is an advantage of getting it all right and doing it right with the proper attitude. So when you take a risk, remain confident and hopeful, trusting that God will be with you the entire trip along your journey. It is so riveting to know how much Life is so Precious.

After, we all have suffered a while and when this part of our season is over. Then will the Lord establish us and bring us out to fulfill those blessings that you have been requesting for, reaching for and asking for. So, rejoice and start celebrating today because the Lord has seen your labor of love and He has heard your cry....

The end of my story, for now!

Notes

Our Lives Bonding Together

Let's draw near with a true and honest heart toward one another, remembering that our lives are precious in the sight of the Lord.

We are all brothers and sisters in unity. Remember to treat each other with respect, with love and kindness, appreciating the kind and friendly gestures that are passed around with love.

"Love heals all types of wounds and scares; it also has enough power to change an ugly situation into a beautiful situation."

Unity brings about strength, boldness, satisfaction, happiness, and the will to do anything your mind and your heart has tapped into, to achieve.

Positive words turn away wrath and anger. Mean and grievous words stir up the unnecessary anger that we do not need to entertain at all.

Coming together as a complete culture from all walks of life and all kinds of backgrounds does prove that we can conquer anything.

Treating people like you want to be treated is key and vital to everyone. No one deserves to be mistreated at any time or looked down upon regardless of what the excuse or the cause may be.

You can be rich or poor, you still need the Lord in everything that you do. Rich people can lose their minds like a poor person does.

"Next time, when a homeless person is close by, next time a mother at the grocery store doesn't have enough money to put food on the dinner table, next time a family who just cannot pay their rent or their mortgage, pitch in and let them see your heart by spreading your love."

I have experienced trouble first knocking at the door and then trouble trying to knock down the door. Having me wrapped up, tangled up, and tied up until I made up my mind that I would not lose. *I am going to win.* And I did win!

Jesus says, whenever we do unto the lest, we are doing it and giving it, unto Him. Whatever is done in secret, He said, he'll reward us openly. It other words, we will get it back and much more in return, from the Lord.

The measure that we do will be measured unto us again. The deeds that we display will be displayed again.

God would even allow the wealthy to give unto your bosom. He's God enough to do that for us—plus, he's not slack concerning any of his promises.

"We shouldn't ever allow fear, to prevent us from doing anything good."

Do not let fear rule you, overrule you, or overtake you. Stand on your feet, square your shoulders, poke your chest out, and lift up your hung-down head. Look fear in the eyes and say, "The God that we serve will deliver us, because he is able."

Our God, is able to do, exceeding abundantly above all that we could ask or think to ask. He's able to make all grace abound or very plentiful for us. He is our source.

In life, when someone has dreams of big things, those big things come to pass. Those of you who keep having the dreams of small things, don't get mad at the one who dreams big. Believe in yourself, because you can dream for the big things too, and it will come to pass for you as well. There are plenty of dreams to go around for everyone. God will not withhold anything good from you.

To everyone, it doesn't matter how hard the wind blows with enough force to knock you around, it doesn't matter how loud the thunder roars in your life; don't you be afraid, and it doesn't matter how bright the lightning lights up the sky to cause you to lose focus. When it's all said, done, and over, you've got to keep moving, to get to your prize at the finish line, wherever your dreams may lead.

To all of my favorite personal military friends: Keith Funderburk, James Cox, Robert C. Hightower, Anthony Hayes, Raymond Graham, Jarrod Malloy, Glenn Burks, David Lee, Karl Straughter, Deroyce Mccloud, Mo, Hawkins, Michael Manor, Beola Bradley, William Whitten, Rowmell Hughes, Kevin Klauss, Davenport, Tim Vanhook, Dunlap, Susan Walker, Daniel Skinner, Arthur Griffin, Betsy Riley, Terry Seals, David Underwood, Keith Dodley, Craig Best, Yolanda Herring, Ann Obregon, Dinah Davidson, Donna Naupoto, General Griffin, and to all of my friends from the HHB 1/44 ADA. We started out on North Fort and then later moved to the main side of Fort Lewis, Washington, near the Soldier Field House gym and C 220th FA Hanau, Germany. To everyone I met in Lawton, Oklahoma, so good to me during the holiday season with all that good Southern-style cooking. I, Big, and others tried to play some hoop after eating. We all looked like the Three Stooges bouncing and shooting the basketball when we were so full.

***

My favorite places, spots to be stationed: Hanau, Frankfurt, Germany, New England, Berlin, Puerto Rico, Virgin Islands, St. Thomas, Ireland, Fort Lewis, Washington, Fort Sill, Oklahoma, Fort Bliss, Texas, Fort Lee, Virginia, Fort McClellan, Alabama, Fort Knox, Kentucky, the Warrant Officer School in Fort Rucker, Alabama (January 2005).

***

Tacoma, Washington: This was my true beginning of a career in the military. I was able to meet such incredible people—Bishop, Mother Westbrook and family, the entire Kinlow family (Jason, before he even became the best barber, I remember when he used to cut my hair in the bathroom many years ago). Derek Clark, Pat Hill, Neal Jones, Mark Logan, David Hart, Star, Vincent Watson Jr.—you all inspired me to stay strong in the gospel music. Everyone embraced me with so much love, making me a part of the family. Tacoma, Washington, was good to me. I could never forget any of you. We all would attend all the church musicals throughout Tacoma and Seattle. I miss those days.

***

The Bay Area: To all my best friends who where there during the passing of my mom and they didn't know it: Gary, Skip, Fran, Randle, Roger, Will, Terry Brown, Eric, Terry "Magic" Marcus, Russell, Garcia, Arnold, Merl, Frank, Earl, AJ, Marquez, Reggie. Bay area's best gospel influences: Carl Wheeler,

Sylvester Burks, Derrick Hall, Lawrence Matthews, Lorraine, Debra, David Jackson, Nona Brown, Demetrius Tolefree, Tylos Jackson, Rufus Turner, Rico Thompson, Kim Green, Silvester Henderson, Otha Lee, Ray Murray, Reggie Murray, Edwin Hawkins, Joel Smith, Devon.

Index

Closed Doors

When certain doors in your life are closed, it's for a reason. When there's nothing left to learn and it leaves you with no more growth to receive. Don't go and try to reopen those closed doors. God has new doors ready to open for your new purpose. Everyday is new for a new beginning!

A man's gift and a woman's gift too. Will make room for you and your gift will also bring you before great men...

Have a plan and stick with your plan: create a plan of action and the logistics to follow and get it done. Believe to Achieve...